TO
CLAIRE & DAVE

Chilangos in the House:

The True Story of a MexiCAN

I REALLY WANT TO THANK YOU
GUYS FOR BEING THERE
FORE US.

I WANT TO WISH YOU
A VERY SPECIAL WEDDING
AND TO BE HAPPY FOR
THE REST OF YOUR LIVES

Leo Cervantes

Yolanda Navarra Fleming 6-14-16

GRACIAS

Dedication

Leo Cervantes would like to dedicate this book to his mother, Abigail Soto Bello, a true warrior, who has pushed past her fear. Always.

To Jenny, the warrior I married, the wonderful mother of our children. Thank you for everything you do.

Yolanda Navarra Fleming dedicates the book to her husband, Guy, and their children, Vinny and Julia Fleming.

Acknowledgements

Leo Cervantes would like to thank the Chilangos engine: Tatiana Baros, Diana Nevarez, Juan Trejo, Geovanny Calderon, Margarita Osorio and Ricardo Tlaxcantitla, Mayra Barreto, Fredy and Diana Buritica, Father Daniel Peirano and Any Buritica, Ruben Lopez, Tino Caplanson---CPA, Barry Packin, Lori Mayer and Bill Cahill---lawyers, Joanne Betta from Paychex for payroll, Charlie Betta from Pilothouse for credit card processing, Sal Cino from U.S. Foods, Doug Doughty from the Lusty Lobster, Guillermo and Gloria Lopez from American BLG who supply meat, Joe Pace from Jersey Capital, who supplies liquor, and Mark Sharpe---contractor, Sherwin Williams in Middletown, Nancy Hughes, Rosemary Sorrentino, Siobhan Cornelius, Remedios Cobb and Maureen McCrink Gribbroek from Valley National Bank in Highlands, and Stephen Smith, All American Chevrolet in Middletown, Linda Vollbrecht and Steven Stokhamer from Home Depot in West Long Branch.

And also to: Robert Zweben, Nick Kouvel, Edgar Marin, Jacob Varella, Nene Gonzalez, Janny and Marco and the entire Torres family, Ana Maria Gomez, Lupe and Lynn Munoz, Horacio Ontiveros, Tommy Grasso, Rick Korn, Janice Selinger, Danny Shields and Jenn Beck, Frank and Valerie Montecalvo of Bayshore Recycling, Diego Maya, Carol

Cassidy, Julio Moreno, Nancy Ellen Kravis Photography and Daniel Morreale, Carla and Ken Braswell and ShoreGrafx Inc., The entire Gonzales Family, Leila and Michael Terreri, Jay Harmon, Carlos Medina, Luis Rodriguez, Governor Chris Christie and Lt. Gov. Kim Guadagno, Abraham Lopez, Joan Colette, Albeiro Orozco, Belén Marmol, and Javier López.

Yolanda Navarra Fleming would like to thank Leo Cervantes for uttering the words, "Someday I'm going to write a book," and meaning it, and also to Guy Fleming for acknowledging her ability to turn that utterance into a reality. To Jenny Correa Cervantes for being a champion of this work, and Leo's children, Eric, Gabriela and Emiliano for their tolerance and moral support.

Also to Ed Gabel and Ken Braswell for their work on the book cover, to Johnny Carrasquillo for his formatting and publishing efforts and guidance. To Tova Navarra, editor and mother, John Navarra, father and financier, brother Johnny Navarra, sister-in-law Mitzi Navarra and their entire family for their life-long support. And to Leo's family in Mexico: Abuelita (Abigail Soto Bello) and Noemi, Alejandro, Victoria, Eduardo, Omar and Liz for their hospitality and friendship while we visited Neza.

"Remember, remember always, that all of us ... are descended from immigrants and revolutionists."

—Franklin D.
Roosevelt

"You gain strength, courage and confidence by every experience in which you really stop to look fear in the face. You are able to say to yourself, 'I have lived through this horror. I can take the next thing that comes along.' You must do the thing you think you cannot do."

—Eleanor
Roosevelt

Leo Cervantes, owner of Chilangos Mexican Restaurant.

Prologue: Welcome to Chilangos

Since its inception in March 13, 2002, Chilangos Mexican Restaurant in Highlands, NJ has been a favorite not just for the food, but for the heart-warming experience of being surrounded by friends you may never have expected to make. First-timers don't often realize they are walking into Leo Cervantes' platform for everything that is important to him. It's not uncommon for customers to become fast friends. I'm a perfect example. Each time I showed up for yet another delicious meal, I found myself hoping to learn a little more about Leo and what fuels his Mexican mojo.

He's a very giving man of 46, especially when it comes to tequila. He told me once never to say no when asked if I wanted a shot because it usually meant that it would give him the opportunity to have one too. But he certainly doesn't need it to socialize or articulate his ideas. If you can listen past his melodic accent, it suddenly becomes clear that his English is nearly perfect.

Before we began working on the story of his life and times thus far, I used to go to Chilangos and felt let down if he was absent. In other words, eating was only half the attraction. He does what comes naturally to him, which creates the space for free-spiritedness, a live-and-let-live mentality and grounded energy that people are as hungry for as they are his brand of authentic Mexican food.

Leo lives to have fun and create fun, in and out of the kitchen, so it stands to reason that he would want to serve more than the expected traditional fare.

His tagline is "the way real Mexican food should taste," with a dash of whimsy, of course, because he has an ongoing need to create. For instance, Chilangos is the only place one can score *La Quesadilla Perfecta*. A hunk of smoked gouda cheese caught Leo's eye at the store one day and he quickly brainstormed "the perfect quesadilla" by stuffing the cheese into a flour tortilla with chicken, walnuts, agave nectar and chipotle sauce.

If you're picking up this book because you are a repeat customer, you may have heard a story or two about Mexico or Colombia where his wife, Jenny, and waitress Tatiana come from, over a shot of tequila. Or maybe you were the recipient of one of his friendly April Fools' Day pranks. Or better yet, maybe he fed you before, during or after Hurricane Irene or Superstorm Sandy---when eating at Chilangos wasn't an option---at the shelter at Henry Hudson High School, his house or in the Chilangos parking lot.

If you've never met Leo or shared a shot with him, after reading about him, you'll want to. He'll make you laugh and feel like you've known him for a lifetime. If you take the time to talk in depth, it doesn't take long to tap into Leo as a source of motivation. Just about anything is possible in his mind.

Without realizing it, he has been practicing the Law of Attraction from birth because he learned it and so much more from his mother, Abigail, who believed poverty could be a source of motivation for him and his siblings. Poverty only implies a lack of money, not love or friendship, talent, creativity, willingness, joy, playfulness or hope, or any other aspect of life that affords us happiness. His undeniable MexiCAN attitude speaks to his daily routine of exploring his passions, which all seem to revolve around celebration.

About two years ago, many years after our initial meeting, my husband, Guy, and I had dinner there and were saying goodbye to Leo. I don't even know how it happened, but "goodbye" turned into a long conversation about the problems in Mexico. We could easily blame the tequila, but there was more to it. I learned many things, including that *Chilango* is a nickname for someone who migrated to Mexico City from another part of Mexico, although now, anyone from Mexico City is considered a Chilango.

I was fascinated. I wasn't thinking about anything else while Leo spoke. Afterward, I had the same feeling I get after watching an intriguing documentary, or as I refer to it now, Leo-TV. I might never have gotten so lucky to hear the entire story. Standing in the crowded entrance while other patrons were coming and going, Leo said, "Someday I'll write a book."

Having heard too many people blurt this out as a half-hearted intention, I hesitated to respond. I will be eternally grateful to Guy for helping me manifest my destiny with the statement, "Yolanda can help you with that."

He wasn't joking. As a writer, not to mention an amateur psychotherapist, I'd been listening to people's stories since I was a child. I had already written my own (unpublished) memoir and helped several others tell their own stories. At that moment, I was in the process of copy-editing and brainstorming a title for what turned out to be "Memories of the Unexpected: The Story of a Tuskegee Airman," by Milton L. Holmes.

Since I was just about through, the timing was perfect. I was happy to have yet another opportunity to dig for the hidden treasures of someone else's life, so I might learn new lessons and vicariously enjoy experiences.

There is nothing more intriguing to me than the human process in its many variations---the unexpected lows that give way to conclusion, the triumphs, lessons, moments of perfect universal order ---when everything is right and peaceful, and especially the sudden shift in perspective when disguised blessings are unveiled. Whether or not there is a master plan is debatable, but I believe a person's choices and his or her gravitational lean toward either the positive or the negative are what make everyone's story unique.

After we had gotten ourselves put back together again after Hurricane Sandy, I enjoyed the additional gift of traveling with Leo in March 2013 to see where he spent his first 18 years. I'd never been to any part of Mexico before, not even to a resort. Still, because I wasn't going to Acapulco or Cancun, the decision to go wasn't easy.

Several months prior, the mere talk about the trip inspired great concern by my immediate family, who were convinced I would be in grave danger in the midst of Mexico's drug-related crime and a corrupt government, including police officers who were too often educated criminals in uniform equipped with badges and weapons.

It also didn't help that there had been travel advisories in the recent past, warning Americans of the threat of kidnapping and random wrong-place-wrong-time-related crime. Even my world-traveling brother canceled a trip to Oaxaca in 2009 when he was told by hotel officials to stay home because tourists would not be safe. That tidbit along with the uprising of anger displayed by the drug cartels and the threat of bringing back Swine flu as an unwanted souvenir created a trifecta of reasons not to go.

In my case at the time, the question was: How could I leave my family behind and risk being murdered or forced to smuggle drugs? At Leo's request, we sat down as a family to watch his friend Julio Moreno in the movie "Maria Full of Grace," and it officially scared me. At the same time, the rebel in me made me roll my eyes in disbelief that anything bad would happen. I also knew better than to think Leo would be willing, never mind enthusiastic, about putting me in harm's way. But if it was really that important for me to see his country up close and personal, rather than on other people's travelogues online, I was warned by loved ones that I should wear drab clothing and keep my long blonde American flag of hair tucked under a hat. Better yet, I should dye it black to blend in.

After weeks of debate, especially with my husband who was petrified to lose me to the cartels, I dropped the idea of going because my intuition stopped me in my tracks. Something didn't feel right. Leo had already booked his flight and decided to take his young niece in my place.

Two days before Leo left, we were at Chilangos at the end of yet another uplifting and informational interview for the book, and the kind of lunch that left me feeling full and privileged--- chicken in *pasilla* sauce with tortillas, rice and beans, and a salad sweetened by agave nectar. For dessert, we shared a piece of pumpkin flan Jenny had made. While passing the spoon back and forth, I said, "I feel like there's some bigger reason I'm not supposed to go to Mexico."

Leo shot me a serious look as he often did when his wheels were spinning. "I hope it's not something bad."

He would be gone for a week and I was left to work on the book, sorting out our conversations, without the benefit of my own Mexican experience. It haunted me.

About two days before Leo's return, flashbacks of what's now known as The Perfect Storm of 1991 when I lived on the Manasquan inlet loomed large. Another storm was predicted, which meant preparing for the house to be flooded, or not. During Hurricane Irene, the water didn't get high enough to damage the house and we were grateful.

This time, Mother Nature whipped up a special blend of summer and winter weather forecasters called Superstorm Sandy. The night before the storm we would stay with our friends Lori and John Quigley (also big Chilangos' fans) up the street, assuming high tide would be the worst of it. The full moon and high tide rose about 11 feet higher than usual, and although slow-moving, it was one of the nastiest hurricanes ever to blast the country with rain and 75 mph winds. We were among the thousands of residents forced to deal with major flood damage.

Leo returned the day before Chilangos would be destroyed. His house was safe, but the restaurant was devastated, even though he did everything he could to put a positive spin on it. It was a terrible thing for us to have in common. This book-in-progress would be shelved until my home and his business were both rebuilt, which at times seemed unlikely to ever happen. The importance of going to Mexico became even clearer to me, knowing all too well that unexpected events can change reality as we know it without much warning, if any.

Fast forward to the end of March. The Interjet flight to Leo's country, which he left as a young adult to find a better way, but loved enough to return often, was surreal. I had no expectations, but was prepared for an eye-opening adventure.

Leo's older brother, Alejandro, was standing in the distance at the airport when we arrived.

Leo pointed him out and told me to say, *"Hola, Gordo!"*

I knew it wasn't particularly nice to call someone Fatty, but apparently, in the light-hearted Cervantes family, it was considered a term of endearment. He laughed out loud and set the jocular tone for the entire five-day visit.

The most immediately noticeable difference was the tropical weather as we waited for the rental car. The overall plan was to have fun because that is Leo's typical main objective, even in the context of work. For me, it was equally important to witness the level of poverty that fueled the family's fire to be healthy and well-adjusted in spite of everything.

By day two of the trip, I was motivated to let my guard down because I believed I was safe, which made me hate my frumpy-on-purpose clothes and wish for prettier things to wear in this pretty country. Mexico presented me with a sense of beauty and vitality I felt compelled to reflect. My only difficulty in embracing Mexican culture was the language barrier. I didn't wish they spoke English, but that I spoke Spanish.

Leo poked fun about how many shootings, killings and drug deals we might witness on any given day. He pointed out the Federales of the United Mexican States, who appeared nearly everywhere we went. He attributed it to the efforts of President Enrique Pena Nieto of the Institutional Revolutionary Party, the new president, elected July 2012, and the government, now committed to picking up where Felipe Calderon, his predecessor, left off in his six-year battle against the drug cartels.

I felt dirty considering my country's part in the equation and often thought of the word Ameri-CAN'T, as in "can't" stop contributing to the crime in Mexico because of our instant gratification-addicted nation. The U.S. is the largest consumer of drugs trafficked in Mexico and responsible for supplying the cartels with weapons. Equally atrocious is the human trafficking from Mexico into the U.S. (for illegal drug sales and the sex trade) that supports crime organizations with as much as $2 billion per year.

This kind of activity requires cooperation between our countries, and I can only imagine if efforts of the same magnitude were channeled for the greater good rather than mutual destruction. Leo and I consider our collaboration on this book a way to spread awareness for the sake of both the

United States and the Mexican United States, of both the joy and atrocities of Mexican culture.

I had already met Leo's mother, Abigail, also known as Abuelita (dear grandmother), while she was visiting Leo in New Jersey, but it was even more fun to see her on her own turf.

Meals filled many of our waking hours and I took pleasure in the flavors and textures, not to mention the calories, of dishes whipped up in Abuelita's kitchen. I sat at the head of the large dining room table where my first meal was chicken enchiladas and pig's feet in red sauce. The truth is I would have eaten anything put in front of me and expected greatness, but I didn't anticipate the resemblance of Abuelita's homemade tortillas to my mother's famous crepes. And I wondered aloud, *How am I supposed to eat those white flour discs from the store after this?*

Dessert that night was homemade fruit pops that trumped any cake I'd ever eaten. And since we had stepped out of the frigid temperatures of New Jersey winter into the warmth of Mexico, the exotic flavors---tamarind, coconut, pistachio, pineapple, mango and banana---surpassed decadent.

The same big bowl of pickled cactus, carrots, peppers and cauliflower presented at this meal made a second appearance for the next day's breakfast, as well as the rice, beans and enchiladas.

Because I love dinner for breakfast and breakfast for dinner, I was more than happy about that. However, in my honor, before the real food came out, breakfast began with an assortment of bakery treats, served with *chocolate-caliente* (hot chocolate) with cinnamon, which I must have obviously met with low-level horror. Reading my apparent fear, Abuelita promised I would gain only one pound per day.

Abuelita is a cheerful, comfortable-in-her-own-skin type of woman in spite of having raised her children in poverty. She emerged from those obstacles with hard work and a bit of tunnel vision, and now lives in a much larger, more refined, yet still modest version of Leo's childhood home.

As the family's convenience stores provided each family member with a job, they all contributed to each other's well-being, and the house that was once a creative piling of raw materials---through a series of renovations over the course of several years---became the cool, clean and comfortable home it is today. Abuelita lives in her own section of the house (when she's not in the U.S. visiting Leo or Eduardo) with Alejandro and his family.

In Mexico, it's common for people to have businesses either directly in or attached to their homes. Such is the case for Alejandro, his wife, Victoria, and their three adult children, Lisette, Omar and Eduardo; all put time in at Chilangos Internet Café, which is attached to the family's home in Neza. Abuelita has her own apartment also attached to the house, with her own kitchen and living area, where on display is the same sewing machine she used to design and make wedding gowns when Leo was a child.

Omar gave up his bedroom for me, which Lisette, the oldest, had recently painted. Their younger brother, Lalo (short for Eduardo) repeatedly helped me connect to their WIFI account.

Even though six of them shared the house, the lack of tension was both mysterious and refreshing. I've had the experience of living with grandparents and great-grandparents, with still-fresh memories of my mother and her own mother butting heads. This is not to say that there are never disagreements in this little portion of Mexican paradise, but there is a palpable respect and therefore peace that keeps the family engaged.

Oddly enough, I awoke every morning to a rooster's crow, perfectly within the realm of Mexican normalcy. City dogs were everywhere, crossing streets with astounding awareness and perched on roofs. Colorful town markets offered groceries, and clothing, and special treats like *camotes* (sweet potatoes) in honey (also used to make a special toffee-like candy that originates in Puebla).

I was honestly not alarmed by freshly killed chickens on countertops in the market or other animal parts. Everything I tasted was some degree of delicious and the varieties of peppers seemed endless. We stuck to eating authentic Mexican food wherever we went, and I noticed more *taquerias* than anything else, where they serve small soft tortillas filled with everything from beans and rice to meat, cheese and vegetables.

Even in the midst of poverty, I sensed people were focused on their daily tasks rather than causing trouble for others. The streets of Plaza Garibaldi, Puebla City, Taranda in Guanajuato and Basilica de Guadalupe, even past midnight, were full of fun-seeking parents with their children, groups of friends and young lovers. The only time I felt slightly unsafe was in the passenger's seat of our rental car, where we spent a lot of time sight-seeing, and sometimes getting lost. My trust in Leo's driving, what I knew of it from what I'd experienced back home, was unflinching. However, what I didn't expect was for just about every trip to remind me of a New York City cab ride. Imagine a succession of speed bumps every few miles and traffic lights thought of by motorists as mere suggestions!

Sometimes we stopped, but other times, it just didn't make sense if no one was coming the other way. Leo's mantra was, "This is the jungle!"

One day, we drove several hours to the state of Guanajuato—a more relaxing trip on long stretches of highway with a lot less traffic, and no speed bumps or traffic lights. We were going to see Leo's cousins Esperanza and Francisco on their farm, where Leo and his family would visit his mother's parents when Leo and his siblings were small. The landscape offered easier living, a polar opposite of Neza, with farm animals on every property, a bounty of fresh food and stretches of mountain views. All the homes were made of similar concrete, some painted different colors, and many with storefronts. I was sure that visits to this state, if only for the change of scenery, gave them the necessary break from the "jungle."

Esperanza and Francisco were completely self-sufficient because of their vegetable farm and supply of animals—pigs, goats, cows and chickens. Francisco had lived in Chicago eight years prior, but preferred a simple life on the farm. They made a living growing agave plants and selling the fruit to a tequila maker, as well as candy, snacks and drinks, among other things, in their small convenience store. The store was attached to their modest home not far from a river, where donkeys and horses could be found at the water's edge. We ate one of the freshest meals possible–homemade tortillas made on a comal (large flat surface pan) over a flame of mesquite, pine or whatever wood they could find, fresh cheese, beans and rice, cooked cactus, avocado and salsa.

After an evening spent walking in the field to the river to watch the sunset, and talking in the street until after dark, we went to the home of an old family friend, the daughter of "Mama Juliana," who had often taken care of Leo while his mother worked. They preferred to have us stay with them rather than find a hotel for the night. The room I slept in was right off the kitchen, with a large wooden dresser. In the wee hours, I heard scratching coming from inside the drawers and didn't know what to think. When we opened them in the morning, we met their baby chicks being kept warm.

The next day, I met a petite old woman introduced to me as "Mama Juliana" as she was perched on a wooden chair in her fenced-in yard, wearing a lime green sweater in the heat. Her hair tied back revealed a face weathered by the sun in the fields and drained by all the people she had cared for. I had an odd feeling when I saw her face, like she could be the 87-year-old Mexican version of me. She was a mirror of sorts, but I didn't know why. She squeezed my hand, which was the same size as hers. She was hunched over, clutching her cane. I didn't let go of her hand or she of mine. Instead, I sensed her years of not being touched, so I used my massage therapy education (acquired in 1996) and gently kneaded her shoulders and back. She spoke quietly in Spanish and Leo translated. She said I must be an angel sent from heaven to help her.

Leo told her I was a healer, a kind of doctor, whose touch could ease her pain by increasing her blood flow. The fact that she was comfortable having a complete stranger who did not speak her language touch her gave me a glimpse into her beauty and strength.

Her laugh lines revealed years of joy and she talked about the beautiful children she'd cared for over the years, including Leo, and the only man she ever loved, her husband (15 years her senior), who had died 26 years prior.

Apparently, she had recently had a benign tumor removed, yet was still convinced she was dying. She knew it would be her final year on earth. When we met she was in the process of winding down. So many thoughts rushed through my mind while my hands were on her until I became sure we had something in common. I prompted Leo to ask her birthday and was amused to find out it was January 6, the day before mine. Now my recognition made some sense. She was also a nurturing and deep-thinking Capricorn who tended to put others first. Leo told me of her passing early this year in 2014.

"Mama Juliana" and Victoria (Alejandro's wife) in the yard in front of Juliana's house in Guanajuato.

There were so many subtleties I would take home from Mexico, not the least of which was utter embarrassment for buying into the notion that Mexico was a modern day Wild West. Instead, and to my surprise, there were more police cars per square foot than I'd ever seen anywhere.

While the Cervantes family could have easily been crushed under the pressure and gloom of their immediate landscape, there was no anti-depressive aid or support system other than the natural ones they created among themselves. They were blessed to have such as a positive outlook and ability to do the sort of mental gymnastics required not to give up. But they don't believe their rise above the negativity was spectacular or miraculous. They didn't have a choice but to be stronger than the thorns in their sides. Their will to survive pushed them to the other side.

It is interesting to me that Leo, more so than the rest of his family, looks back in awe of their collective rising above their lack of resources. Perhaps he appreciates it the most from his perspective as the youngest child watching the older ones struggle. The nurturing spirit Leo developed is a combined result of his father's absence and his mother's presence. Revisiting the past in such granular fashion is Leo's way of celebrating the process and using it to motivate others.

His story has become a significant part of my learning process and personal growth, absorbed during more than two years of research, traveling to Mexico with him twice by now, and countless hours spent digesting his melodic accent while drafting his life story. I have been pleasantly surprised to discover that we share the same values, which resulted in many electrically charged moments during the interviewing process. In talking and sharing experiences that we have felt others could enjoy, learn from and possibly gain motivation, we have committed to a continuation of our shared process with the people who surround us in a live format. Please look for our web series where we will document our efforts to educate, inspire, motivate and enlighten anyone who cares to watch.

The opportunity to find out, firsthand, the value of life from the perspective of a MexiCAN like Leo, has truly broadened my view of the world and gives me hope on a daily basis. I would love to know that you share in the evolution of that hope because in my estimation, there is no truer or more valuable gift. As Leo told his stories to me, I wrote them down and now give them to you.

Yolanda Navarra Fleming

January 2015

Happy Birthday to Me

It was September 6, 1987. It wasn't unusual for me to be home alone in the late afternoon. Everyone was out working. My shift at the family store began at 11 p.m. My 18th birthday might have been like any other day---an empty house until later in the evening, except that my friend Pépe came to visit and wish me well on the day I officially became an adult.

His aunt Francisca, was a successful business owner who helped my mother open a convenience store. By this time, we owned three stores. Turning 18 should have been a bigger deal, but none of us could do much more than focus on taking care of business and this day was no different.

Pépe and I were both crazy happy guys with a lot in common. We both attracted girls with our dark good looks, but he was short and hated it. We spent plenty of time together and even took the same bus to and from work every day. Because we talked nonstop and liked to poke fun at everything and everyone, we could have been a comedy team. I appreciated my good friend being there on my birthday, even though all we did was talk and watch TV.

When it was time for him to leave I walked with him to the corner bus stop about 20 feet from my brand new tan stucco house, which now had new furniture and appliances on the inside, and pink and red bugambilia flowers on the outside. My family's reward for working hard as a team was having the nicest house in the area. It didn't bother me that birthdays weren't big events. I was glad to have a refrigerator.

We were in the middle of talking as we waited for Pépe's bus when a big dusty black Crown Victoria pulled up alongside us. We watched quietly as two of the passenger doors swung open. The driver stayed behind the wheel as two big tough-looking men in their 40s got out. They each had a gun and pointed them at us.

One of them said, *Get in!*

Pépe and I were scared, but stayed quiet as we got into the backseat of the car. The gunmen sat next to either of us pressing the guns to our heads making sure we wouldn't try to escape as the driver sped away.

They said they were undercover police looking for rapists.

Are you the ones we're looking for?

I said, *No*, and pointed to my house and said, *This is where I live*, as we passed it. Then we passed my school and I pointed that out.

I said, *I also work at my uncle's mechanic shop. My friend came to see me because today's my birthday.*

The man with the gun to my head said, *Oh! Happy birthday.*

They frisked us and asked if we had any weapons or drugs, which at that point meant marijuana because anything else was too expensive and unavailable. They took Pépe's two or three dollars from his pocket. I didn't have any money, but in my lower right pocket next to my knee he felt something. *Whoa! What's this? Take them out.*

It was a cheap pair of sunglasses. He looked at them and said, *Oh they're very nice. Would you give them to me? Can I have them?*

I said, *Of course you can have them*. And he said, *Thank you, you're a very nice guy.*

Pépe asked, *Are you real cops? Where are you taking us?*

He kept talking and annoying them. I wished Pépe would play it cool and keep quiet so we had half a chance of celebrating my next birthday. But he was so nervous that he kept talking until one of them said, *This little guy is tough. Let's teach him a lesson.*

It was now dark. We drove about three miles to a main street I recognized even though there were no street lights or moonlight. We passed a taco stand and about four blocks later, the driver stopped the car. The man next to me got out of the car and said, *Get out!*

I knew there was a cemetery near Los Rosales about six blocks away. We looked back and I could see the light bulbs hanging from the window of the taco stand. One of the men pushed up his sleeves, pulled his gun and told us to turn around. Pépe and I looked at each other wondering what was next.

He said, *I'll give you to the count of three. Run!*

We started running toward the taco stand and my body was so tense that I could feel the bullets on my back, even though they didn't shoot. I ran as fast as I could toward the light and when we got there, we turned around and the car was gone.

We couldn't speak. Pépe and I stood there sweating and panting. As we started walking, Pépe fished in his pockets and found he still had a few coins so we could take the bus. We went across the street and waited for the next bus. By then we could talk even though we were still in shock. On the bus I saw a guy helping the bus driver collect money. I recognized him from school. When he saw me he said, *What are you doing here? You don't live around here.*

I said, *You don't even want to know what just happened to us.* Then I told him the story. He said, *You guys are lucky to be here.*

There were many shootings during the time. Police were looking for a bank robber and fugitive named Alfredo Rios Galeana, who was nicknamed Mexico's Public Enemy Number One because of all the crimes he had committed. He was an army deserter and a police officer and had accomplices who were also being hunted by the police. It wasn't uncommon for groups of people to be taken in and interrogated by the police about Galeana. When they suspected someone was holding back information, they used torture to force it out of them. It actually happened to some of my friends and I was scared to death at the possibility of that happening to me. That fear changed my life.

You can't really say you know a city, even if you've lived in it for years, until you leave and live somewhere else and have something to compare it to. I know Mexico because I grew up there, and even more so now because I left.

At this point, I've lived in the U.S. longer than I lived in my native country. I realized I had to leave Mexico when I was 19 because I wanted more than the city could offer me at that time. I was taught to dream and by then, I believed my dreams were impossible to create in my home country. That may not have been completely true, but that's what I believed and my perception was my reality.

I didn't only see things from my own point of view. The fact that many of my friends wanted to leave inspired me to want to do the same, also because the ones with no thoughts of leaving had no real goals or motivation. Some of them had already chosen a life of crime because they didn't know anything else. It was common for young men who aspired to be criminals to join the police force and hide behind a uniform, which made it easier to steal from people and practice corruption.

There were also a few people I knew who had money and opportunities, but many people were more like me and didn't consider crime an option. I had been watching and learning from my Mom—a hard-worker, who looked for and created opportunities for herself. For instance, she was a talented fashion designer who offered her services and poured her creative energy into designing and sewing unique clothing, like wedding gowns. She also opened three convenience stores and employed all of us.

My mother inspired me and though I left, I have never stayed away for long. While traveling back and forth between the U.S. and Mexico City, I have watched it evolve. The drug cartels still pose a problem for the government because they are so powerful and almost impossible to control. But it seems that Mexican people are fed up with the situation and are working toward cleaning up the country. The government is less tolerant than ever of crime and the overall safety of my city has improved, even though the cartels have not and probably will never go away. But I have to admit that the idea of crime served a purpose in my life. It inspired me to work hard because I didn't want to resort to that kind of life. I wanted more for myself and my family.

Mom's sewing machine at home.

Leo at age 10 and Abigail at age 12 in Neza.

Childhood Survival

My mother tells me she thought I was going to be a kickboxer because I was so active before I was born on September 6, 1969. She says I slid out like a bar of soap at 1 a.m. I was the fifth child–the baby of the family. They named me Leonel Cervantes Soto.

My hometown of Nezahualcoyotl was built on a drained bed of Lake Texcoco. Neza (for short) was named after the king of nearby Texcoco, as well as the poet name Nezahualcoyotl, which means the "fasting coyote." It was fitting for us because my father, José, was a frustrated poet.

My mother's sister and her husband, who owned the mechanic shop, bought land in Neza when my parents still lived in a small rental in Magdalena, Mexico City, where my mother's parents had met and got married years before. Magdalena was a farming town with animals and crops right in the middle of the city. My parents may not have wanted to move there, but they wanted to be closer to my aunt and uncle, and rented a room.

Once Alejandro, Noemi and Eduardo were born, they bought an empty 30x50-foot lot because that's all they could afford—a lot in the middle of nowhere. They chose the best piece of land they could buy, which my mother still owns today, for 15,000 *pesos*. Their mortgage was 130 *pesos* a month. That was back in 1967, two years before I was born. To give you an idea of how much that was, 130 pesos now only buys two packets of Chicklets gum.

My mother, Abigail Soto, was born in the very small village of San Lorenzo on July 23, 1941, under the astrological sign of Leo, which is kind of funny, although I'm not a Leo at all (other than my name). I'm a Virgo, which means I appreciate the combination of hard work and originality. It's true! But Mom is a typical Leo---ambitious, confident and independent. When she was little, her father took her to the fields to teach her to work on the farm. They didn't have water or electricity or any services at all. Her father (my grandfather) Fidencio Soto, was a farmer who grew all different crops, but mostly vegetables. My grandmother, Antonia, had 14 kids, but seven of them died from various illnesses.

In 1956, when Mom was 15, she went to Mexico City. Her two older sisters were already there and the oldest needed my Mom to help take care of her kids. At 17, Mom got a job as a maid in a house for a doctor and his wife, Amelia, who recognized Mom's positive mentality and potential to get out of the vicious cycle of ignorance that people get into. She was tough on Mom because she wanted her to learn. Mom and her family were too poor to go to school because as soon as they became old enough, they had to work to support their families. Amelia encouraged my Mom not to be a maid for the rest of her life.

My father, a Libra, was born September 25, 1940. He came from the city of Dolores Hidalgo, Guanajuato, although I don't know much more about his background. I do know, according to a little bit of research, that Librans are very intuitive almost to the point of being psychic, indecisive or slow to make decisions, which he was, and usually have a hot temper. But he was also a good man. I believe he was always afraid to make the wrong decision and cause more trouble than he was already in.

Amelia was such a strong influence on Mom that she had more to say about their relationship than my grandmother. It wasn't enough that Dad was very handsome, and Mom wanted good-looking kids, or that he was tall compared to other guys she knew. Looking back now, Mom admits it was a physical attraction more than anything else that brought them together, and even though he was a good guy, he wasn't outgoing or goal-oriented, which she thought she could change.

I have good memories of my father when he was around. He used to hug me, call me "Leoncito" and carry me on his shoulders. Things were only bad when he drank and became somebody else. He and Mom would fight, she says, because he was insecure and felt intimidated by her. It scared me; I hated it so much I'd run and hide. Dad must have hated it too because he would run and hide in his own way. He didn't have a car to drive, so he'd get on the bus and go away for a while, sometimes for weeks, and everything was calm again. I don't know where he went or how long he'd be gone, but he always came back eventually. I used to watch other kids with their fathers and think about what it would be like to have a father who played ball with me or to help me with my homework.

Aside from their fighting, I respected my father because he never hit us or used bad language. But now I believe if he had not been depressed and had more of an outlet for his talents, he would have been happier. It also didn't help that our town of Neza was a very depressing place where everything was so primitive we needed optimism to survive. Without it you could get into trouble, like my Dad. There were only a few other houses in the area, and the land was otherwise bare---no trees, sidewalks or even pavement. My parents couldn't afford to have a house built, so they used to buy cheap materials like raw concrete for the floors and cardboard for the roof. They built a tiny house of three rooms without a foundation or a façade, by themselves. When it rained, water dripped into the house. The only reason we had electricity was because we ran our own line. There were no services, not even garbage pick-up. We would dig a hole, put the garbage in it and burn it. But not everyone did that. After a few years, we had more neighbors who dumped their trash about 100 feet from our property, which became an official dump that grew to almost a foot high and about a quarter of a mile long.

The bathroom was inside, but you had to go outside to get there. We were just like the impoverished families you see on the TV commercials for World Vision, except my mother could afford to buy some food sometimes. When she had the money, she'd go to *El Mercado* (the market) twice a day since we had no refrigeration, once in the morning and once before making dinner. We finally got a gas stove and a refrigerator when I was a teenager, but before that, she cooked on a petroleum stove.

At our poorest, we survived on rice and beans. There was a time when we literally had nothing. Mom broke down about it once and only once when I was about 5 or 6. My Dad was not there. and my mother was frustrated. She was only human and felt bad at times, but more often she wanted to teach us how to be tough. Turning a negative into a positive was one of her talents. She said, *C'mon, kids. Today we're going to play a game. Let's pretend we're camping in the middle of nowhere. We're on an adventure and we don't know where we are. There's no food, so we have to hunt for it. It's a survival game.*

Then she asked, *What would we do if we found three tortillas, a lime and some salt? How would we survive?*

And we all said, *We'd eat it.* So, she said, *OK, then, let's do that.*

When we were doing a little bit better, we'd have chicken once, maybe twice a week, and very rarely, pork. We also ate a lot of eggs, cactus and potatoes. Beef was too expensive. I never thought we didn't have enough to eat because of the magic my mother worked in the kitchen. With only a few simple ingredients, like rice, beans, onion, tomato, and tortillas, she could make something delicious.

We had no real furniture, except for a wooden table that Dad made, which bothered me because it was wobbly. I thought we should have a better one. Within our three rooms, the five kids (Alejandro, Noemi, Eduardo, Abigail and me) slept in one room in two cheap queen-sized beds, one for the boys and one for the girls. Mom and Dad slept in the other bedroom. But when I was very little I remember sleeping with them.

Every night we all said, *"Hasta mañana, Mama, hasta mañana, Papa, hasta mañana todos, Que sueñen con los angelitos."* That meant: Goodnight Mom, Dad, everyone, dream with the angels. Everyone said it except Eduardo, who would just say, *Igualmente,* which means "same thing," in Spanish.

Neza was a jungle where almost everybody was uneducated and poor—the perfect recipe for raising kids to be gangsters. The advantage of growing up there was that it was the best school for survival. It gave me the tools to become a happy, motivated, sharing, caring person. It may sound crazy, but for me it was true.

As positive as she is, Mom doesn't like when I talk about how we grew up because she feels that she failed us and didn't do enough. Yet, she remembers us as happy children who didn't need to be entertained. We had to learn to keep ourselves busy. There was no organization---no soccer team, no baseball team. Kids played with broken bats in the streets. No one had money to buy things like that. Being poor was a stage of our lives. It was like a catapult. It was a good thing, according to Mom. I don't know how I felt about it then, but now, I believe it. It was the beginning of something. You have to start somewhere, usually from the bottom. That's what happened to us. There was garbage across the street, but we were always cleaning and trying to make it better. Mom treated cleaning like exercise. She'd say, *See this pile of bricks? Let's move them over there.* If any of us complained, she'd say, *It's good for you.* Now we know it was more of an excuse to keep us busy and off the streets, which was unhealthy not just because there was trouble there, but because of the garbage dump. It was more than just an ugly thing to look at. When it rained the puddles had reddish living organisms swimming around in them, which we called *microbios.* There were lots of flies and dead animals on the streets, even dogs. It was a lot for anyone to overcome, especially a child.

The benefit of my life was my Mom because she had vision. As a seamstress, she made clothes and sold them. She made most of the clothes we wore. People who came to visit thought we were rich because of the creativity she put into making the house look better than it might have. Because there was no façade on the exterior of the house, we found used tires at the garbage dump, dug holes and planted them halfway in the ground and planted flowers around them, like a fence.

Another smart thing she did was to camouflage the compressed cardboard ceiling. She collected burlap flour sacks from the bakery and cut the tops and the bottoms to make sheets. She soaked the sheets in lime powder and water, and sewed them together. My father hung them on the ceiling and it looked like Sheetrock. We were poor, but there were poorer people than us. We had land and a house. There were people whose houses were made entirely out of garbage, and others who had no house at all.

Dad had creativity and did smart things, too. He didn't really cook, but he liked to make tortillas. A Mexican engineer named Guillermo Gonzalez Camarena invented color TV, but we couldn't afford it, so Dad invented a way to make our black and white TV screen colorful with cellophane paper. He thought he was being funny, but it looked nice. First, he covered it with a red piece, but he didn't like it. It was too red, so he tried blue. Dad's real talent was writing.

Mexico is so fascinated with death that we have a holiday to celebrate it. My Dad loved it. The tradition called *Day of the Dead* starts at the end of October and lasts until the first days of November. Death is considered part of life and making offerings to the dead was a way of inviting the soul to come and enjoy life one last time. When someone died, they'd have a table with all kinds of things on it according to what the person used to like when he was alive–things like food, clothing, pictures, cigarettes and tequila.

Another ritual practiced during *Day of the Dead* was called *Calavera*, which means skull in Spanish. People used to write fake obituaries that rhymed to make fun of politicians or celebrities. My Dad would write them and then read them to us. They were so good they could have been on the radio. My father didn't do as much as Mom would have liked him to do. He was more of a thinker. He also loved music like I do. A lot of times, I'd see him writing things down that he kept to himself, and later I discovered they were poems and song lyrics. If he had motivation, he might have been a songwriter, rather than keeping his writing private.

There's a Mexican song that says life is like a beautiful rose. In order for you to enjoy it, you have to grab it even though it's going to stick you. But you'll never know the beauty of that rose without touching it and feeling the pain it inflicts with its thorns. In other words, you have to experience the pain to appreciate the beauty.

At two years old, I could have gotten killed in the jungle of my childhood. I don't remember it happening, but my brothers told me the story. My father was working a night job while Mom was in the house about to design the first wedding gown she would ever sell to someone in town. She needed time to work, so she told us to go play.

We were outside on the street when a Volkswagen Beetle ran out of gas right near our house. The driver left the car to go look for a gas station. All of us kids and some of our neighbors were playing with the car, pushing it back and forth. The road was uneven. Alex, who was eight at the time, and supposed to be watching me, didn't notice that I tried to grab the car like everybody else. When they pushed the car back it hit me, I collapsed and the tires ran over my face and broke my nose. My brother pulled me by my feet out from under the car. He ran inside the house, crying. I had blood all over my face. My mother took me on the bus to the nearest clinic about 20 miles away, where I had to stay overnight. She went back home to take care of my brothers and sisters, and to get clothes for me.

The next day, the nurses gave me a shower and wanted to feed me, but I refused to eat anything because my Mom was not there. Later the nurses told Mom I asked for coffee. She finally got there and fed me. My Mom saw that I was fine, and asked the nurse why she was told on the phone that I was going to die. Apparently, someone must have told her that to teach her a lesson.

Dad was working a security job at night. From work he went to the wrong hospital looking for us. When he finally got to the right hospital and found out what had happened, he cried like a baby. It was a lesson for all of us. The guy looking for gas came back, put the gas in his Beetle and left, without ever knowing it had run over a child.

The next time I escaped death was the following year. I was three. A lady named Angela rented a small room in the house next door to us. She was poorer than we were. She had a child, Zotero, who was about my age, and she and Mom were friendly. One day, she wanted to take Zotero, and her older daughter, Dolores, to *El Mercado*, and asked if she could take me with them. We took a bus from the corner and got off a few miles away.

Inside the market, Zotero and I spotted some toys and stopped to look at them. Angela didn't notice we had stopped, and kept on walking. When Zotero looked up and noticed his mother wasn't there, he panicked and started crying. He took off trying to find his Mommy. He was afraid. I stood there, trying to think about which way to go. I sort of knew where I was because I had been there before, so I went outside and started walking in the direction of our house. I knew if I kept walking toward the garbage dump, I'd get to my house. On the way, I had to cross about 20 streets before getting to a main street. I looked both ways because I had learned from living in the jungle to be aware of my surroundings.

When I walked in the door, sweating and exhausted, I asked Mom for a drink of water, then went into my room and went to sleep. While I was sleeping, Angela was still at the market looking for me. Her daughter, Dolores, took the bus to my house to tell my Mom that I was missing.

Something tragic just happened, she said. *The kids got lost. We found my brother when they made an announcement on the loud-speaker. I don't know what we're going to do because she's still looking for your son.*

What are you talking about? Mom said. *He walked in about 30 minutes ago. He was very tired. He's sleeping.*

The girl went back to tell her mother that I was safe.

It's amazing I didn't get hurt another time when Public Works came to fix the streets and left a concrete pipe for us to play on when the workers weren't around on weekends. My brothers and I pretended to be superheroes. I was Superman. Superman flies, but I found out I don't.

When I was five years old, I started kindergarten at the home of a woman who decided she wanted to teach. About five of us from the neighborhood went to her house together, about two and a half miles away. By the time we got home from school around 3:30 p.m., my brothers and sisters and I were exhausted, so we'd take a little *siesta*. I used to cry to see them all lying down because I needed attention. I still don't like to be alone and prefer to be in the presence of somebody. When I drive, I like to be by myself so I can think, but that's the only time.

Every day, my Mom gave us 25 cents. We had the choice of buying either a one-way bus ticket to or from school. Sometimes we got up early enough to walk to school, so we could save the money and buy juice or candy.

One day, my brothers had spent their money on treats, but I still had mine and they wanted me to share it and buy candy for all of us. When I said no, I started running away and they chased me. They were laughing and I knew they were playing, but I also knew I was going to have to share my coin with them.

A few blocks later, I turned my head to see if they were still chasing me. When I turned back to focus on the road, I noticed a big motorcycle with two young guys on it about to make a turn. I tried to stop running, but the little pebbles on the road made me skid and I landed on my butt with my legs straight out. I watched the motorcycle's front tire roll over my legs. I looked up to see the guys' faces looking down at me. When I noticed the second tire, I started crying wondering what was going to happen to me. I felt even worse because I knew it was my fault for running away. My brothers caught up to me, picked me up and said, *Don't cry. You're going to be fine.*

They rubbed my legs, saying, *We were just playing. We're going to buy you a juice.* They asked me if I could walk. I was so scared because I couldn't feel my legs. I tried to get up, but my legs didn't respond. After 10 minutes, I calmed down and sucked on the juice my brothers bought me. Slowly, I was able to walk. My brothers said, *We shouldn't tell Mommy because she will worry.*

It seemed like there was always something to worry about. When we got sick, we worried that we were going to die because we had no money to see a doctor. Once when I had a fever Mom started crying, which made me think she thought I was going to die.

My uncle had a friend who was a doctor, so we took a bus late that night, hoping he would be there. We had no phone to call first and when we got there we found a note on the door. The doctor was away on vacation. We were sitting outside. Mom was hugging me because it was cold. While she was crying, I looked at her and I willed my 5-year-old mind to be strong, to show her that I was OK. I didn't want her to suffer.

I had a next-door neighbor named Arturo. His family was poor, but they had a black-and-white TV. We went to their house one day and his mother, Rosa, was crying. Arturo came out of his room and was saying crazy things and laughing at a TV show we were watching. He seemed delirious, repeating whatever we said and laughing. I wasn't really paying that much attention because I was distracted by the TV.

The next day, my brother picked me up from school on his bicycle. He said, *Listen, man. There's something I have to tell you, but I don't want you to worry about it. Arturo died this morning.*

I said to my brother, *So he's in Heaven with God?*

He said, *Yeah. So we have to go to the funeral.*

He had a disease diagnosed as purpura that starts with fever and makes your hair fall out and your skin flake. There were also purple spots on his body about 2 to 3 centimeters long. Within three days, he was gone. We were about the same age. We went to their house where Arturo was laid out. In those days, it was the godmother's job to dress the dead child. Mom was Valente's godmother, so she made a funeral dress for him of green and white satin. I remember seeing him, pale and dead, lying in a pretty white satin wearing the gown she made, and brown sandals on his feet. There was cotton stuffed up his nose and in his ears. His eyelids were dark purple. I knew I wasn't going to see him anymore.

Days later, his two cousins, Valente and Abel, who were also the same age and lived a few blocks away, got the same illness. Valente died about two or three weeks later, but my sister Abigail and I couldn't go to the funeral because we were also sick. We were in two different beds in the same room. Abigail's case was worse than mine. Her skin was flaking off and her hair was falling out in clumps. Within three days she had bald spots on her head.

I remember being in bed for four or five days, knowing I would die just like Arturo and Valente. I felt like my brain was being cooked. I was sweating. I was boiling hot. My Mom went on the bus about a mile away to find a pharmacy. She told the pharmacist we were sick and he drove her back to the house in his car so he could give us shots. I saw the needle and when I turned over in bed to I could feel it piercing the skin of my buttocks. I remember my Mom holding me tight. Days later, I started feeling better. Again, I had to show that I was strong because my mother was crying.

Trying to be strong became a theme that followed me through every stage of life. So many times I've had to do things I didn't want to do, but knew I had to do. Dad had a night job as a security guard at a sewing factory in the center of Mexico City near the Mexico City International Airport. It was a huge building, like a sweatshop. Sometimes, he'd take my sister and me, the two youngest, with him to work to spend the whole night. We liked to go because they had a green rotary telephone and a radio in the office and a couch where we would sleep. We'd call the radio station and request songs, like *Sinfonia Bajo del Mar*, which means symphony under the sea.

One night as my father put sheets on the couch, we were having a great time listening to the music and singing along. But before going to sleep, we went to the store to buy milk and snacks like Twinkies and bread. We looked forward to waking up in the morning to watch the planes from the driveway as they prepared to land.

As we walked back from the store a few blocks away, Dad said, *Oh my God, I left the keys inside.* He wasn't supposed to leave at all, but being locked out could get him in a lot of trouble, maybe even fired. Within a few seconds, he remembered there was a small window that was always unlocked. He begged me to climb through the window, go upstairs to the office and get the keys. I was little and the place was so dark and horrible and scary that I said, *No way, Daddy, I'm not doing it.* He said, *You have to. You have no choice. I will talk to you. You'll hear my voice. You're going to be fine.*

I was crying and shaking as he pushed me through the window feet first. He held my hand as I landed softly on the floor of the dark factory that was as big as a Home Depot. As I walked through the dark, I bumped into big tables and chairs. The only thing guiding my way through the long hallway was a big statue of the Virgin of Guadalupe framed in red and green neon lights. I got to the scary statue, and then climbed the long staircase. I was dying inside. I got the keys, went back and gave them to my father, crying like a baby. I *was* a baby. That's why I think I'm still afraid in the dark. To this day, I hate it so much. I wish I was normal.

In 1977, when I was about 7 years old, my Dad started drinking. He became verbally abusive when he drank. When he was sober, my mother would ask him why he didn't spend more time with the family and less time with his friends and girlfriends. When he was drinking and insulting my Mom one day and the next day asking forgiveness, she lost respect. She wanted to give him the opportunity to say he was wrong or to admit they were finished, but she was disappointed and eventually didn't care what he did. She focused on herself and us, which made the lack of a good marriage matter less.

She taught us about responsibility very early. Each one of us had an assignment. She would say, *Together we can do it. Let's do it. Teamwork!* She was our life coach. She was so positive she didn't even want to hear about the negative. Her goal was to keep busy, off the streets and out of trouble. One of us would sweep and someone else had to mop. I would go with Eduardo to buy the bread. Eduardo always made the coffee.

She didn't allow us to talk like they talked on the street. At home we had to speak properly and couldn't say bad words. There were a lot rules–good ones, not difficult ones. They all had to do with making sure we were headed in the right direction, growing and learning. It was also important for her for us to learn to read and write. She had friends and was always motivated. That's why she was so annoyed at my father for lacking motivation.

When they had no money, Mom suggested he go to the U.S. to work and send money home. Sometimes he said yes, but then when the time came, he didn't want to go. So Mom told him, if she had the opportunity to go, she would do it. So he said, *Then, go!*

My Mom was invited by a family to go to Texas to work in a restaurant in San Antonio to bring some money back. I remember I was sad the day she left, but I don't remember details. They crossed the border in their car at a checkpoint. Mom was using someone else's green card.

My Dad didn't believe she would actually go, but while she was gone for three months, he took care of us. My Mom's mother, my Abuelita, stayed with us while Dad went to work and left when he came home. While my father didn't have the same vision my mother had, he was a good father in his own way. At that time he wasn't drinking at all, and I knew he loved us. My mother's time away gave him a chance to show us. He would say, *Let's make some tortillas.* He'd get the flour out and roll them. I missed my Mom, but even though she wasn't there, I felt protected. I was proud of her and also happy knowing she had the chance to see something different. It was as if she went to war and was protecting us from far away. She went there for us, not for her. It also gave me hope that maybe I would go to the U.S. someday. My Mom did it, so why couldn't I? She sent money back, and that year was the first time in my life I remembered having a birthday cake.

Abuelita came over and we had cake with blue icing. She made hot chocolate and everyone sang happy birthday to me. According to my mother, it was my father's idea to do that and then write to her to tell her we set a place at the table with hot chocolate where she would have been sitting. He didn't want my Mom to worry about us while she was gone. She assures me I'd had birthday cakes before, but that was the first one I remember.

Working gave her a sense of purpose, but it wasn't a perfect situation. She says, *I wasn't able to eat anything but the figs off the tree behind the restaurant until I made money two weeks later. If you wanted to eat at the restaurant, you had to pay.* She was there to make money, not spend it. Being away from us wasn't easy on her. She remembers sitting on a bench at the bus stop, wondering every time she looked up at the sun or the moon or stars if we were doing the same thing.

The owner of the restaurant in Texas was so sympathetic to Mom's situation and her determination to make money to send back to us that he offered to marry her so she could have us move there, too. But the manager felt threatened by Mom, who was a quick learner and hard worker, so she called Immigration and reported her. Before Mom had a chance to take the owner up on his offer, she was deported after only three months.

She was happy to go back home, but she didn't accomplish what she had set out to do. The person she was living with told her to go back to Mexico, see that her kids were OK, and if she wanted to come back, they would do everything in their power to bring her back. But once she returned she didn't have the same motivation to go back. Instead, she decided to leave her experiences in the U.S. behind, fix our house and make her life the way she wanted in her own country.

I wasn't one of those kids who had fun going to school. I was nervous about it and I was shy, which nobody believes now. In fact, I was so shy that girls used to ask me if I was gay. I was not, but at the same time, I wasn't the typical guy going crazy for the girls either. I wasn't the popular guy at school, but it didn't bother me. My first girlfriend lived far from my house. I had to walk a mile to take her home from school first. If I didn't want to see her, I used to have to hide because she would come looking for me. I was more concerned with whatever I was doing at the time to make money, like selling bread.

There was a guy who made a brick oven in his house for baking bread. One day, he decided to send kids out to sell it for him and they'd make a 10-percent profit. Pretty soon, he had about 20 kids selling his bread. My friends and I heard about it and started working for him. We also sold *gelato* (Italian ice cream) on the streets. I used to make 50 *pesos* a week. Whatever I made, I gave to my Mom. We had to work because we did not have material things, or even some essential things like toilet paper and napkins, so we had to do whatever we could to bring money home.

One summer Dad decided we should sell *mezcal* on the street. It was a plant, like a huge agave, but more firm like pineapple.

You cook it and caramelize it to make it sweet. It would have made more sense to sell it in the colder months because it was more of a cold-weather treat. When my aunt heard that she said, *What is wrong with him selling it in the summer?* But it may have made sense to him somehow because he also sold *gelato* in wintertime.

My mother's oldest sister married a man from Guanajuato. They moved to the city and he learned to be a mechanic. They went to the U.S., made some money and then came back to Mexico and opened a mechanics shop. Then he opened another one. He was my Great Uncle Felipe. He made a lot of money and they bought rental properties. But once they had money, they went crazy. We lived in the garbage while they had houses and cars and businesses. He helped us by giving us jobs at his mechanics shop.

At 9 years old, I was cleaning car parts. It wasn't too pleasant, but it was a good experience and I learned what it meant to work hard. It was a dangerous place for kids to be; there was a fire once and potential danger every minute of every day. We worked hard, and in his mind, he was creating men. I appreciated it, but he was very tough on us, sometimes even abusive. They were very ignorant. They came from nothing.

Another uncle, Uncle José came to my house to talk to my Mom. While he was inside I thought about how I wanted to drive. I thought I knew how from watching other people drive. In the middle of his conversation with my Mom, I asked for his keys to get something I left in his car. He kept talking and handed me the keys. I went outside and thought, *This is my opportunity*!

I got in the driver's seat and even though I could barely see over the dash, I started the car and took off. My friends were outside playing ball. I passed by and shouted at them and waved so they could see me. I came back, parked the car and no one knew!

My oldest brother, Alejandro, was Uncle Felipe's mechanic when he was about 17. I knew how much he cared about me when he told me he would buy me a brand new blue bicycle if I did well in school. That might be the only year I really tried to do my best. Alex would have liked to have had a bike when he was a kid, but he didn't, so he wanted me to have one. So he and my grandmother put their money together and bought it for me. It was beautiful. He still remembers how big my eyes got from excitement and how I couldn't even speak because I was so happy.

We didn't have a gym or a football field, but we weren't too poor to have fun. In fact, we knew how to enjoy ourselves just playing with peach pits as if they were jacks. We didn't need expensive toys. In spite of all the things we didn't have, we were happy. Like most kids wherever you go, we played games in the street. We used to play football (known as soccer in the U.S.) with friends. All you needed was the street, which was not paved, four bricks for the goal, a ball and a bunch of friends. There are things money doesn't buy. We were always in the street, playing. These days, you don't see that here. Now everything is controlled. There is a difference between poor people in the U.S. and poor people in Mexico. You don't see people playing football. You don't see people walking and talking. In a lot of places, you don't know who your neighbor is. The U.S. is a beautiful country, but there's something missing– the warmth of people.

There was another game that could be played by two people, named after *bolillo*, a kind of Mexican bread (like Portuguese rolls, but thinner). We took a stick from an old broom about 10 inches long and scraped the ends with a knife until they were pointy. After cutting another yard of the stick, we dug a hole for the *bolillo*. One kid would try to lift and throw the smaller stick with the yard stick. If one player didn't catch it, the other player threw the *bolillo* and hit it with the small stick, then that player had to carry the other one to the stick.

There were two games we played for coins—marbles (*Canicas*)---and another game called *Tacon*, which means heel of a shoe. First, we drew a circle about five feet in diameter. We started with one *peso*. Five guys would each take a peso and toss it in the circle to see who got closest to the edge, and that player would go first. With another peso, you had to toss it to try to hit one of the coins in the circle without stepping inside the circle. If I threw it and hit the coin just right, to make it fly out of the circle, I'd get to keep it.

Thankfully, we all had some escape from the city and the garbage and the stress of living there. My crazy Uncle José, the youngest of my Mom's siblings, used to take us places. When there wasn't room for all of us, he'd say, *Don't worry about it*, and open up the trunk for me and my cousins to get in. We could have died from the fumes, but somehow we were OK. My uncle was a crazy, happy guy. The few times we went to a swimming pool with him, he would say, *C'mon, I want you to learn how to swim.* But he would throw us in the water and I was afraid of that. So every time he offered to take us swimming, I'd say I didn't want to go.

The best vacation was one we took once a year. Mom would take us for the long walk that took several hours to visit my great-grandmother and great-grandfather on their ranch in Guanajuato, which we called *El Rancho.* For us, it was an Indiana Jones adventure and we loved it.

In El Rancho, my grandfather, Nicolas Soto and grandmother Piedad, had an adobe house with a dirt floor. Nopal cactus plants (prickly pears) grew everywhere on their acres and acres of land. Even though they owned a lot of land, they were very poor. But they were a different kind of poor. Everything they had, they either grew or made. They grew corn, tomatoes and beans, all kinds of peppers, strawberries, peanuts, watermelon, honeydew melon, cucumbers and zucchini. Haas avocados, which are the best avocados for making guacamole, come from that region of Mexico. Everything was fresh. Everything was homemade. Everything was beautiful.

They had ways of living healthier than we did. In the morning, we'd milk the cows and have fresh milk, and make cheese. They had a place to go fishing and they could grow food.

In Neza, I don't think we could have planted anything because the soil was mud. But we had eucalyptus trees. The smell of it always reminds me of my mother making a mixture of eucalyptus and Vicks VapoRub in a pot, and making a tent out of a blanket for me and my brothers and sisters so we could inhale the eucalyptus. It made us feel better when we were sick.

Once while visiting the Hot Springs near El Rancho, I had to pretend to be Superman again. Even though I was 11, I didn't know how to swim because we never had a place with a pool or any water around us. I stayed away from my crazy Uncle José, so he wouldn't throw me in the water. Everybody was having fun until all of a sudden I saw a kid fall into the swimming pool. Nobody noticed because it was so quick. Everyone else was too far away from us to help. I didn't know how to swim. I was afraid of the water, but I had to do it. I jumped into water over my head, and grabbed the kid out. He ended up being OK.

I had another water-related incident the first time I went to Acapulco when I was 12. Before arriving at Acapulco Bay, we stopped and jumped in the river. There was a 10-year-old kid crying. People were asking him what was wrong.

The mountainous view in Guanajuato, taken from outside Esperanza and Francisco's house during our 2013 visit.

Yolanda made friends with the family's pigs in Guanajuato.

He said his father jumped in the water and wasn't coming out. He was drowning. They finally pulled him out of the water, but there was no rescue team. I was looking at the kid and his father, thinking, *this poor kid*, and I was only like two years older. He was all by himself. I said, *Please God, help this guy*, but he died.

After that, we went in the water. There were large, smooth, slippery rocks in the river and I stood on one of them. While talking to my cousin, all of a sudden my feet flew out from under me and I hit my head on the rock. I was unconscious for a few minutes. My cousin shook me and said my name until I woke up. He said, *You scared me. Your eyes went white.*

At 18, Alex got another job working for a racecar driver. They traveled all over Mexico. He had to go away a lot, but he made enough money to buy us a refrigerator and a stove, which I appreciated. It was hard for me having my oldest brother and my father gone. Sometimes Alex left for two or three months at a time. He was busy working, but he was also escaping the pressure of Dad not being around. Alex felt responsible for supporting us. He also knew what it was like to pretend to be Superman.

One of the only times my father came with us to Guanajuato, I was only 8 or 9. We had to cross Rio Lerma to get to El Rancho with some of the workers from my Uncle Felipe's mechanic shop. We walked into town where people were drinking. I noticed my brother Alex's speech changing as he was getting drunk. I had to push my father, uncle and Eduardo to leave. When we went back to the village, I was the one in control. By the time we got to the river, my brother was so drunk he jumped into the river. I started crying out of frustration because I was scared and couldn't do anything about it. There was a guy crossing the river on a ferry and I asked him to please help me because the river was known for swallowing people up and I thought Alex could drown. My father and the other guys were far behind us. I was with my brother, keeping an eye on him. They couldn't see us because they were about 300 feet away and there were bushes and trees blocking the view. I was daydreaming, imagining how my Mom would react if she had to find out he drowned. There were parts of the river that were shallow, and others that were deep and I was thinking about a couple of years before that when my distant cousin, Carlos, who knew he had a heart condition, and jumped into the river to rinse off. I wasn't there to see it happen, but he had a heart attack in the water and died.

Somehow my brother swam and got out. At the time I didn't realize that he not only wanted to escape temporarily, but maybe permanently. Now I do. The pressure he was under made him do many crazy things that I not only forgive him for, but feel sorry he had to go through.

Once when he was 20, Alex came to school to pick me up. We were on our way to get on the bus, but he decided to stop into a cantina along the way to talk to one of his friends. I stayed outside for about three hours waiting for him to come out. He had gotten drunk with his friend. I didn't remember until he reminded me not too long ago when I visited him in Mexico. He felt so bad about it, so it was good to talk about it.

In spite of everything we went through, my mother planted a sort of microchip in me that made me believe we were gifted. She used to say, *Being poor is the most beautiful thing in the world because we get to dream.*

And each time I've had to do something that required me to be like Superman, I felt better about myself–and stronger. Even though I had fear, I learned to hold on to the confidence that I have what it takes to conquer it. I guess Mom had to do the same thing and that is most likely where I learned how to do it.

As Dad became more frustrated and less in control of his own life, he started trying to control Mom. He got aggressive sometimes, though he never hit her. He didn't want her to work or leave the house, but she realized it didn't get her anywhere to give in to him. He would ask her why she was wearing her hair a certain way or wearing make-up. He complained to my grandmother once that Mom didn't respect him. He said, *She doesn't listen to what I say*. But she didn't change her behavior because she didn't believe she was doing anything wrong. If she had, it might have made things worse.

In the beginning, my mother could see that he wasn't motivated. My aunt could see it, too, but Mom thought once they had kids, he would get motivated. But that's not what happened. Instead, he maintained his relaxed attitude about raising the family. It didn't help that he was really tall, good-looking and she was in love with him. What made her fall out of love with him was when she used to tell him they needed more money; he'd suggest cutting back on meat and milk. As it was, we only ate meat once a week and Mom watered down the milk.

She'd say, *It's not about us; we have to take care of our kids.* He'd say, *What do you want me to do, go out and rob a bank?*

Of course that's not what she wanted. In fact, she proposed they start a business to capitalize on her talent as a seamstress. She would make clothes all week to sell at flea markets on the weekends. But he didn't see a need because in his mind, we were comfortable. He didn't understand my mother's desperation. He didn't see our not having shoes as a problem. It makes me wonder whether he had shoes when he was a child, or if he drank watery milk or didn't have meat more than once a week. Believe it or not, I don't know what his childhood was like.

There was a gang in Mexico City known for stealing sneakers. Why sneakers? Kids don't want to wear just any sneakers. They want to wear whatever is popular at the moment, usually the

most expensive ones, so they were high in demand and easy to sell on the street.

There were times when I was desperate enough to do something I might regret, but I believed whatever I did would affect my Mom and she didn't deserve that. Even though we were poor, I also believed there was something else, somewhere else and chose not to focus on what we didn't have. I didn't have good sneakers, but it didn't matter.

Leo (left) at age 11, sister Abigail (middle) at age 13, holding a real piglet, and brother Eduardo (right), age 15. It's not easy to see, but Leo's foot is poking out through a hole in his right shoe.

Living in the Jungle

Although there is extreme poverty in Mexico, there is also extreme wealth. Mexico is the second largest country in Latin America. There are about 120 million people dancing around the 32 states and the federal district of Mexico City, the capital, where there are more Spanish-speaking people than anywhere else, even Spain. Mexico is also the 16th largest exporting country in the world. Mexico has a lot to offer other countries as one of the biggest producers of silver and electronics, including most of the flat-screen TVs sold in the U.S., medical devices and aerospace parts.

Who knows what some brilliant MexiCAN is inventing right this minute that will revolutionize the world? My family may not have invented anything original, but we were creative in the business of survival and weren't afraid to try new things. We had no choice because we came from nothing and lived in a sort of jungle that could have swallowed us up if we weren't careful.

We had a little bit of everything, but we also needed a little bit of everything. Sometimes we were hot, cold or hungry, but when we couldn't afford to pay the bill and lost power, we made it fun by sitting together and telling stories about El Rancho.

When my parents were first married, they cooked on a kerosene stove until I was about a year and a half old. Eventually, my mother was given a gas stove by one of her customers, whose clothes she washed and ironed. Mom made all of our clothes when my brothers and sisters and I were small. My first store-bought shirt came from a family trip to Chapultepec Park when I was about seven. At the time we all liked the TV program "El Chavo del Ocho," so Mom and Dad bought us shirts advertising the show, whose title meant "The Kiddo from Channel 8." It was a unique Mexican sitcom that's still on TV today. We could identify with it because it was about an orphan nicknamed El Chavo (kiddo) and other characters in a low-income housing complex.

By the time my mother could afford to buy me clothes, I needed a suit for the sixth-grade dance. I wasn't excited about it because we were not allowed to choose our own dance partners. Cecelia, the girl I wanted to go with, was cute, but the teacher paired me up with a girl I didn't really like. She was too quiet, too chubby and didn't have a very pretty face. I was only 12, but I knew what I liked.

The whole sixth grade bought the same dark green suit for a group discount. I remember getting dressed, thinking I didn't look too bad, although I wasn't looking at my feet. When Mom looked me over, she noticed my toes sticking out of the hole in my right loafer. Very calmly and matter-of-factly, she said, *We have three choices: You can wear your shoes, no shoes, or your sister's boots.*

I had to crunch my toes to make them fit, but wearing my sister's boots was the best option. I was able to buy my next pair of new shoes with money I earned cleaning car parts. For the warmer weather I bought cheap plastic sandals because I walked so much that my shoes never lasted long.

In 1980, we found out about a beautiful thing that was going to happen to change our surroundings. The 1986 FIFA World Cup was coming to Mexico and a brand new stadium would be built in Neza on the site of the garbage dump. We were so excited. It opened in 1981, even though Mexico was not awarded the World Cup until 1983. The stadium was first called Estadio José López Portillo and eventually became known as Neza 86 for the World Cup tournament.

Cleaning up the neighborhood to build the stadium that now holds 28,000 fans and a nearby shopping mall was great because it created jobs for us. Since my father wasn't more involved in supporting the family, even though I was the youngest, I felt as equally responsible for earning money as my brothers and sisters, who all contributed. She never asked, but most of the money I made went to my Mom. At the time she thought it was a good thing for us to learn about chipping in and working as a team, but when we talk about it now, she says she felt bad and only took it because she had to. I remember her thanking me for understanding what we were all trying to build together.

My best friend Abel had an older brother who was hired to clean the offices for the architects and people who worked for the stadium. One day, he got promoted to work on a digging machine, so they told him to find someone else to clean the offices. He offered the job to Abel, who invited me to work with him. He and I were only 12 years old, but we had learned from an early age how to clean, so it was no problem.

Abel's brother also needed a replacement for washing the employees' cars. When I offered to do it, one of the architects who drove a Volkswagen Beetle said, *You have to be able to drive. Can you drive?*

I said, *Yeah.*

He said, *Prove it.*

So I got into his Beetle, started it and drove around the open space of the construction site. It wasn't that hard because there was nothing for me to crash into. Even though my Mom was only concerned about us keeping busy and staying out of trouble, I was always working to impress her. When I got the job, I couldn't wait to get home to tell her the news.

I said, *Mom, I'm driving. I want you to come see me drive.* She couldn't believe it and was curious to see for herself. So she walked to what used to be the garbage dump, which was now an open field, and met me there the next day so I could demonstrate my new skill. I still remember her standing in the distance, holding an umbrella to shield her from the sun, watching me with her mouth hanging open. She could hardly believe it. The surprised look on my Mom's face made me feel very proud of myself.

I didn't know from the time I was small what I wanted to be, like some people do. All I knew is that I felt very creative and motivated to make things happen. I was open and anxious to experiencing anything that came my way. I also had confidence in myself and felt that I could do anything. I believed that a long time ago and it has stuck with me to this day. I learned so much by observing. That's exactly when I started learning how to be what I have become: A creative, hard-working, entrepreneurial dreamer who makes things happen every day. Mom's openness to different opportunities changed our lives and taught me to be the same way.

When Mom met a woman from the neighborhood named Doña Francisca, they discovered they had something in common--- husbands who drank and left them to raise their families on their own. I believe my father drank because he was depressed, but Doña Francisca's husband was a party animal. He took off with the maid, leaving her and their five children to fend for themselves. Good thing she wasn't afraid to work. She made part of her small house into a store and worked around the clock. Her day started at 4 a.m. when she went to a huge market called *Central de Abastos*, where trucks from all over Mexico stocked up on merchandise. There she bought the milk, bread and other merchandise to sell at the store. She'd return home in time to get her children off to school by 7 a.m. and then opened the store to customers.

As her business grew, she bought a second store, and a short time later, a third. Now she has trailers, warehouses and owns more than one home, all in Mexico City. She recognized Mom's MexiCAN mentality and offered to give her enough merchandise to open her own small convenience store. When they found a store for sale in the neighborhood, Doña Francisca financed it and stocked it, which was a smart move because she was making a new future customer in Mom, who would eventually be able to pay her for merchandise.

If Mom had any trouble, it was changing gears from making clothing to working in the store. Even still, it only took about one year for Mom to repay Doña Francisca, even though it wasn't the best location. Luckily, it was a job that made it possible to finish renovating the house, buy a truck, and buy another piece of property for the second store, which Mom built from the ground up. Eventually, we leased a third store from someone else, including the merchandise.

The store was named ANEAL for all of our names---Alejandro, Noemi, Eduardo, Abigail and Leonel. The whole family was involved, except my dad. One of my jobs, at age 11, was to tend the store. I was good at counting money, giving change and helping people find what they needed. But it was stressful getting up at 5 a.m. and eventually, managing employees. It was also my job to shop for whatever supplies we couldn't get from Doña Francisca. When I got a little older I drove the pick-up truck twice a week to Central de Abastos for the best deals for canned food, soap, vegetables, fruits, bananas, candy and gum because we sold a little bit of everything---even alcohol.

We had to be careful of the police since I was driving underage. The legal driving age was 18, but I never got caught, which is very lucky because I drove all over the place since my Mom didn't drive at all. She never wanted to. I didn't like driving without a license, but here's another example of the corruption. If you wanted a driver's license, you could buy an application without having to take the test. If you didn't want to pay, you had to take the test. If you got pulled over without a license, you had to pay anyway, so it almost didn't matter.

Growing up in the jungle wasn't always bad. But what I am mostly grateful for is being born into a culture with good food. Have you ever wondered why Mexicans seem to belong in the kitchen? It's a cultural thing. Food brings families together and when it comes to our culture, family is very important. You could say the same about a few other cultures as well. Many Mexican parents taught their young children to do simple things like shuck corn or clean beans. I started learning when I was 5. I peeled fava beans. My Mom needed help, but she also wanted to share her enthusiasm for our culture and especially the food, so we were interested.

Watching her cook was like watching a painter paint. When you have a passion for something, you just go with it. She was a natural professional cook, born with the ability to make magic in the kitchen. Without realizing it I learned that creativity is key. Being open-minded about infusing different ingredients together makes the difference between a cook and a chef.

It was also common for people to raise animals to be killed and eaten on holidays. At Christmastime, people usually had live turkeys and chickens. I hated watching them run around after their heads had been cut off. But it makes sense if you understand the essence of Mexican food is freshness and a relationship with the food that doesn't necessarily translate in other cultures.

We grew vegetables and raised pigs, which meant we knew we were eating well-treated and well-fed animals. In our culture, the animals---in our case, the pigs---were part of the family until they grew big enough to be slaughtered. I remember Don Francisco, my friend's father, who had a ranch with horses and cows in a rural part of Mexico, the state of Jalisco. He had a reputation for his knowledge about animals and people would call him for help.

He showed us how to slaughter a pig and cook it over a fire pit. When the pig's legs were tied together so it could hang from the rotisserie, the poor thing would cry. Don Francisco taught everyone how to use a knife to find the location of the pig's heart because eventually, someone else was going to have to do it. He took the knife, aimed with the point, pushed the knife with the other hand into the pig's heart and the blood poured out. The knife was moving even when he let go.

When the pig died, it was time to prepare it. As he peeled the skin back, he explained that the pig had a beautiful life, but on this day it had to die to provide for us. Then he taught us about each part of the pig's anatomy and how we could use it. The shoulder was smoked. The skin was used to make *chicharon* (pork rinds). Then there were *patitas* (pigs' feet), loins and pork chops. When the intestines were removed, cleaned and laid out on the table, we salted them, tied them up and used them as casing to make *chorizo* (sausage). There's a different use for everything. Even the blood was collected and used to cook with. We'd invite people over to enjoy the feast that always included *guacamole* and tortillas to go with our freshly killed, freshly cooked meat.

You can put a Mexican twist on anything if you add certain ingredients and consider technique. There are traditional Mexican cooking techniques, such as *barbacoa* (barbecuing) and wrapping food in various other foods to cook and absorb their flavors. For example, food can be wrapped in banana leaves (*hojas de platano*), cactus paper (*papel de maguey*) and corn husks (*hojas de maiz*). There's another more primitive method of cooking that entails digging a hole in the ground, filling it with coal, placing the meat on top and covering it with banana leaves to create a sort of grease trap of burning wood and steam to flavor the meat.

One of my favorite dishes at the time was *picadillo* (not unlike chili) made with ground beef, *cerrano* peppers, tomatoes, onion, carrots, potatoes, and cilantro. Another was pig's feet. When I go to Mexico, we sit at my mother's big table that seats 10 and have pig's feet cooked three different ways. One is pickled. Another is *franchese* made with eggs. You cook them for an hour in a pot with avocado leaves, bay leaves, onion, and peppercorn, and boil them until they're soft. Then you dip them in flour and egg, and pan-fry and cook them in either tomatillo sauce or the way my Mom makes them with *aderezo* sauce, a tomato-base with garlic, onion and cilantro, which is also the sauce I use now for burritos.

A vegetable I love called *huazontles*, which is like broccoli *rabe*, is dipped in egg and Chihuahua cheese and fried with different sauces. Mom made mole, a rich sauce made of chili peppers and dark chocolate that originated in Puebla or Oaxaca. I was thin, but I used to eat like a monster. I remember eating it and thinking, *Oh my God, I love this.*

My grandmother was at my house talking to my Mom. I went to put my plate down, but I looked at the stove and there was more mole (mo-lay), so I put more on my plate. My Mom and grandmother were standing near the door. I was 14 or 15. They couldn't believe I could eat that much. I used to love food, but my mother's cooking was beyond eating to satisfy hunger. It was exquisite. *Succuolento!*

Some Sundays I woke up to the smell of Mom's food. After hours of cooking, she would say, *In 20 minutes I want everybody at the table.* But she could only spend that kind of time cooking on her days off.

There were many Sundays when we worked at the store. My hours were 10 a.m. to 1:30 p.m. because I attended school during the afternoon session from 2 to 9 p.m. I liked working because I enjoyed talking to people and helping them, but I also realized being stuck at the store for too long was not good for me. I needed to be active, creative and constantly interacting with people. I must have had ADHD because it was hard for me to sit still and read or be in one place for a long time, which made it difficult for me to do well in school.

Once we were running the stores, I rebelled against school. I wanted something more, though I didn't know what. One of the best students named Jesús, asked, *You're a nice guy, so why are you so rebellious?*

One day the social studies teacher came in and collected homework from the 46 students in the room. Our assignment was to fill in a map of Mexico. The teacher was very tough on everybody. I was about the ninth student alphabetically, and that day, because he called the list backwards, I thought I could do it while he was collecting the others, so I tried to hurry. I had knots in my stomach when he came to my desk, held up my unfinished homework and said, *See, this is what I'm talking about. There are a lot of people who wish they could sit in this chair and be here to learn, but instead, we have people like this.*

I wanted to say, *You don't know my life. You don't know what I go through.* But I didn't say anything. Everybody was laughing and I was humiliated. We had an hour of class, then a 30-minute break, then the second hour of class. During the break, I was furious and I went looking for a friend I had known since first grade for moral support. When I found him I said, *Let's go. I don't want to be here. Let's get out of here.*

My friend said, *What do you mean let's get out of here?*

The school had four high walls and a gate for protection. No one would be allowed in without identification and nobody could leave school without permission. But my friend and I waved and said, *See you later,* to the people behind us, and climbed out the window onto the landing and jumped down from the wall into the grass. We went to a nearby arcade to play Pac Man and Street Fighter. No one ever said anything to me about it and I didn't get in trouble.

Another social studies teacher came to me at some point later and said, *Cervantes, you and I know you are not doing very well. We both have a problem. My problem is that I have a pregnant wife at home and money is tight right now. I feel that you and I can have this conversation. If you'll help me, I can help you.*

It was upsetting to me, but I knew that if I didn't do it, I wouldn't get anywhere. So I talked to my friends about it and we all gave him money to fix our grades. I am not proud of this. I never wanted to be part of anything like that or grow up like that. I thought about the day I would become a father and the kind of father I would become would never behave like this.

When I was 13, my Dad finally made the trip to the U.S. with the intention of making money to support us. A neighbor of ours was going and he invited my Dad to join him, and together they crossed the border illegally. I don't know where he crossed the border or what he had to go through to avoid getting caught by Immigration, but knowing all the bad things that can happen, I'm pressed he made it. He stayed in the U.S. almost two years and during that time he only sent Mom $120. If she hadn't been such a hard worker, I'm not sure what would have happened to us.

I would think Mom would still be resentful that he didn't take better care of us, but she's not. Now, she says she wouldn't do anything differently and that her life has been perfect, knowing what it's like to be hungry as well as what it's like to eat good food. She believes it's necessary to do without so you can appreciate when you do have things.

In Mexico, we celebrate Christmas with the Three Kings, who come on January 6th, rather than Santa Claus, who shows up December 25th. Christmas wasn't as bad as it could have been if Mom didn't compensate for my Dad not being around. We always got something. I remember my sister Abigail saying, *When you hear the Three Kings, don't open your eyes because there is a light so bright that it could make you go blind.* They told us that because our parents didn't want us to see them.

Alex had a used tricycle when he was about two. I never got one, but I still think I was the luckiest one of all the kids because I had a metal toy car with pedals. I had a lot of fun with that thing.

Eduardo found a nice dog on the street and brought it home after getting permission from Mom. He told her he didn't want any other gifts, so she let him keep it. The day before the Three Kings, a car passed by and the dog chased the car. It happened to be the dog's owner. Eduardo cried the whole day because the dog left. Mom went to buy him a Foosball table. Dad showed up out of nowhere. It was a big deal, not just because he brought a doll for Abigail and a truck with a boat trailer for me, but because he brought himself. The times he didn't have any gifts with him, he was usually drunk and ready to harass Mom. Sometimes he would cry and complain that nobody understood him. Then he would leave again without saying goodbye. He would go to work and if he didn't come back later that day, it could either be the next day, the next week or not until the next month. It bothered me more when I was 12 or 13 because a lot of my friends had their fathers around to play baseball and do things with and I was home by myself after school a lot. I didn't understand because to me it was simple. I used to say to myself, *We have a family. We have a roof. We have a table. All we need is for our father to go to work to make money to put food on the table.*

When my parents finally separated for real, there was no difference in Mom's life. All it meant was that Dad stayed away for longer periods of time. They never got legally divorced or even legally separated, although he wanted to. She wasn't against it, but she didn't want to pay for it either. It didn't matter to her either way. She was living her life no matter what and she wasn't going to fight about it.

For all of us, it was better when he left because they couldn't fight if he wasn't around. But it was long before cellphones or FaceTime and we never knew what his status. Sometimes he would make surprise visits. Most of the time, we welcomed him when he came back because he would bring something, like a big bag of oranges or toys. We were little and didn't see it as a weak attempt to make up for lost time.

Now I can understand the problem. My mother was so strong and my father came from a complacent family. His whole family lacked motivation and didn't set a good example for him like Mom had set for me. They weren't bad people, but they didn't see the future. I have learned that the future is only as bright as you believe it is.

In 9th grade I met a girl named Bertha, whose eyes changed color according to what she wore. She was 14 and I was 15. I liked her because even though she came from a broken home, she was upbeat. Her parents divorced when she was little, mostly because of her father's alcoholism. He was abusive and didn't support the family like he should have. Sound familiar? Her oldest brother was from her mother's first marriage. She also had two sisters and Bertha was in the middle.

School started at 2 p.m. and ended at 9 p.m. After school, I used to walk her home, which was in the opposite direction of my house. We used to sit outside her door on the sidewalk and I'd put my arm around her and we'd talk. I was always planning my life out loud. I would talk about things I wanted, like a car. I'd tell her that I wanted to make something of myself, to build a nice house and things like that. Bertha was encouraging and would say, *You are going to do big things.*

I wanted to be famous, but I was shy. One day at school, an acting teacher came to introduce himself. They were trying to implement a class, which never ended up happening. He asked everyone if we were interested in acting. A few people responded and started doing what he asked them to do, like making the sound of a bell or pretending to play an instrument. He had us break into groups and choose a scene to improvise. Since I had neighbors who were gangsters, I decided I wanted our group to act out a scene about gangsters and a guy who owed us money. We set him up at a desk where he was counting money. About three other kids were behind me ready to charge the guy on the other side of the door. I kicked the door open for dramatic effect and they grabbed the guy while I yelled at him. We took turns beating the hell out of the guy. Since we had the permission to act we made it very realistic. We took the money off the desk and yelled, *Don't you ever try to cheat us again!*

I knew I enjoyed acting and being something I was not. Maybe this has something to do with my desire to make a movie and create my own reality show. But more on that later.

Before I was to begin the 10th grade, I had to go to the school office to fill out paperwork to register because Mom was too busy working. But I procrastinated until it was too late. In the end, I decided that school wasn't really for me. I told Mom I was going to take a year off. She argued a little bit at first because she wasn't happy about it, but she let it go. She was too busy concentrating on the stores to dwell on it. So, ninth grade was my last year in school. If I were to look back and point to my mistakes, I would say it's too bad for me that I didn't finish. I'm not sorry I own a restaurant---far from it! Of course, a formal education would have helped me, but it also would have delayed my practical training for what I do now, even though my choices were not designed to be that.

Watching Mom get up every day and fight for survival was fuel not just for me, but for all of us. It in itself was an education. Her creativity as a clothing designer helped pay the bills, but it wasn't enough. She didn't complain about the situation. Instead, she did the best with what she had. It didn't help that Dad wasn't around to work and encourage me to do well in school, but I look at it as nothing more than a set of circumstances. I'm sure there are plenty of children who would rather stay in school than have the pressure of working to support their families. But for me, there was no pressure. I was doing what I wanted to do. I loved my Mom so much and always felt the need to protect her, I grew up feeling like I had to help everybody and be Superman.

Most days after school and spending some time with Bertha, I'd go home by about 10:30 p.m. and wait for my sister Noemi, who was 22 at the time. She had to travel 45 minutes on the bus through horribly dangerous areas from the store to get home at night. No one in my family would be home at that hour. Dad wasn't around. Mom would be tending one of the stores. I worried about my sister because a lot of crazy, gang-related crimes happened and people were often mugged and raped. I was afraid of the dark, but I'd wait outside. If she didn't get home by 11 p.m., I'd walk about a half a mile and wait on the corner where the bus would drop her off. I'd watch every bus, looking for her. When I'd finally see her get off the bus, I would exhale deeply. When we finally hired a girl to take her place, I didn't have to worry about that anymore. It was a relief.

By the time Bertha and I had been seeing each other for about two years, we didn't have the kind of relationship where we needed to see each other all the time, which was a good thing because I was very busy working. She was still going to the high school they built across the street from my house during the same time the World Cup came to Mexico. And after school she would do things like cook, watch TV, and hang out with her girlfriends.

My other sister Abigail moved to Chicago, so Alex, Noemi and I worked at the stores. Working kept me out of trouble, unlike some of my teenaged gangster friends who ended up in jail. Some of them are just finishing 20-year sentences and about four friends I used to play football with and hang with on my street are still in jail right now. It may sound crazy, but in many cases, they weren't bad people. They were desperate people making bad choices. They didn't all choose a life of crime because they aspired to be criminals, but rather because they lacked opportunity. If creating opportunity in order to eat and take care of their families meant doing something illegal, they chose to break the law to survive.

When my friend Rigoberto was already in jail serving an eight- or 10-year sentence for robbery, he was blamed for a crime he didn't commit. A politician had been killed and to avoid a long investigation, they pinned it on Rigoberto, accusing him of organizing it from the inside. Although everybody knew he didn't really do it, they had to blame someone.

Rigoberto was in jail because he and his brother, Rodrigo, robbed banks together and stole enough money to buy cars, houses and businesses. They once robbed five banks in one day and kept the money in the house where they lived with their mother. But some of it was stolen when two people who claimed to be police officers went to the house and convinced the mother to let them in. The men pretending to be cops were actually acquaintances who knew about the money. When they found the thieves in Texcoco, Rodrigo got shot in the head by one of them. Rigoberto went to prison and is still there after 26 years.

One of our neighbors named Ricardo, who was about three years older than I, just last year finished serving about 20 years in prison for bank robbery. He was always in trouble and possibly the worst of all the gangsters I knew. But there was a time when he quit drinking and smoking marijuana, and cleaned himself up a bit. He robbed banks for about three years before getting caught during one of the robberies. When he finished his sentence and got out, instead of enjoying his freedom, he robbed a store and was killed by a cop.

Some kids I knew became cops. In the jungle becoming a police officer helped many criminals get their start. Police cars and badges were tools that made stealing, taking advantage of people and overpowering them easier. Even though people knew the police weren't always worthy of trust, they still tended to trust them.

A good example was Alfredo Rios Galeana, a police officer, who eventually became Mexico's number one public enemy. There were a lot of bank robberies in Mexico City, and he was the head of the operation. Ricardo happened to work for Galeana and became part of his gang. Just like Galeana, they had become police officers to gain power. One day they were graduating the Police Academy, and six months later they were driving new vehicles with all kinds of weapons. Things didn't end well for Galeana, of course. He went to jail in 1986 and escaped a few months later. In 2005, he was found living a completely different life in California under a different identity. He was the pastor of a church, who helped a lot of people in his community, before he was discovered and sent back to prison.

I guess my Mom must have been so busy getting the house built, running the business and feeding us, she doesn't remember much about the crime we faced at the time. She believes things are worse now because of the cartels. There was a drug problem then, but alcohol was more of a personal issue for us because of the way Dad used it to hide from his problems.

In the 1980s, the Colombian drug cartels stopped transporting their drugs to Florida because officials started cracking down on it. Instead, Mexico became the main route, which helped build a strong relationship with the U.S. That's why many religious natives believe the U.S. corrupted Mexico. They have an expression that means the closer they are to the U.S., the farther they are from God.

Things were good for the Guadalajara cartel when they were paid in cocaine by the Colombians to smuggle drugs, that is, until their leader was arrested in 1989. Then Pablo Escobar, a Colombian drug lord known as "The King of Cocaine," was killed by the Colombian police in 1993. He was one of the richest criminals in history.

It's bad enough when adults ruin their lives with drugs. But to me, one of the worst aspects of drug-related crime is how children are kidnapped and used to smuggle drugs across the border. They don't just plant drugs on them and put them in transit. They are killed and cut open so their bodies can be stuffed with drugs, closed back up and propped up in the back seat of cars. When they cross the U.S. border, it's hard to tell they're not just ordinary kids sleeping peacefully on a long car trip.

I don't believe people should use illegal drugs. Period. Education is very important, especially for kids who might not want any part of it if they knew that by using drugs they were financing the cartels and killing people.

I still return to Mexico often to visit Mom and other people I love, so I am still in tune with what goes on. There are still problems, just like anywhere else, but today, there are different, more serious problems, though in other ways, improvements have been made.

Now, education is valued in Mexico and supported by the government more so than when I was in school. The first six years of primary school is mandatory, but you have to consider the 52 million Mexicans living in poverty, which translates to a lot of middle school and high school drop-outs. It makes me sad to see young children loading trucks or selling everything from gum to CDs on busy Mexican streets. I'm sure many of them would rather be in school with their friends. The ones who make it to college are truly lucky because they are rewarded with an almost free education in Mexico, and in some cases, they can earn money for going to college. One of the oldest, most prestigious schools in Latin America is the *Universidad Nacional Autonoma de Mexico* (National Autonomous University of Mexico, UNAM) whose main campus is located in Mexico City. My nieces and nephews, Alejandro's three children, who live in Mexico City have received good educations and have been paid to go to school. Fortunately for them, Mexico is becoming more of a land of opportunity as well, although it's still somewhat difficult to find good jobs that pay well enough to live away from home. If I had been a child whose dream was higher learning, I would not have had the same opportunities students have today.

By my 18th birthday, I was old enough to be able to see a little bit into the future. The way things were going, I had no excitement about the years ahead. I had no plan. If everything happens for a reason, maybe it was a good thing that Pépe and I were held at gunpoint not far from my house by men who claimed to be undercover cops. They said they were looking for rapists and wanted to question us. We did nothing to provoke them. Out of nowhere they came and showed us what it was like to be an innocent victim of a crime. They forced us into their car and drove us a few miles away, then told us to get out. They drew their guns and gave us to the count of three as we ran in the dark toward the light of a small taco stand.

They scared the hell out of me, but they also made me fear what else would happen to me if I didn't do something about it. What else could happen if we stuck around? I knew I had a better chance not only of survival, but success, somewhere else. I had energy, motivation and creativity. I wanted to be happy. I also knew I would not go to college and all I had at that point, other than my family, was Bertha and my job at the store. That's when I decided I had to get out of Mexico.

Leo, age 17, at home in Neza.

Crossing the Border

In Mexico there was so much poverty that only a very small percentage of people had jobs. Those who did usually had connections. I was lucky to have learned the benefits of being poor. I also learned how to look past it, meaning that you can be poor and still have a clear view of things. Not all poor people are dirty, ignorant criminals. Just like not all wealthy people are clean, smart and scrupulous. I learned how to use the hunger and poverty as motivation. Of course, it's not always easy to see the benefits of not having enough money.

A boy named Manuel lived on my street was my friend at one time. As 12-year-olds we sold bread and ice cream together and I discovered he was very much like me in the way he approached life. He wasn't afraid to work and enjoyed a challenge. Even though he had a mother and a father, he was like the man of the house.

Manuel's father was a quiet guy who worked for Corona beer and after work, he organized an adult baseball team that played every Sunday. If they played and lost, they would drink and get drunk. He they played and won, they would drink and get drunk. If they played and tied, they would drink and get drunk. One day when we were running down the street we saw some guy who looked unconscious lying on the ground. After we passed him I realized it was Manuel's father, who must have been drunk, got off the bus and passed out as soon as he took his first step.

Manuel was very responsible. He lives in California now and just became a father for the second time. We used to talk about what it would be like to experience the new world, a place where we could achieve goals and have our own businesses.

As a teenager, he was invited to join a gang of criminals. He turned down the offer because he knew it would only be a temporary solution that could turn into a permanent problem. Eventually, his mother moved to San Francisco to help support the family. Of course, Manuel wanted to go, too. Manuel's grandmother was a U.S. citizen and his father's boss had written him a nice letter of recommendation when he applied for a visa. I'm not sure if that's the why he had no trouble getting it, but no matter what happened, he was very fortunate.

When I first applied for a visa, I wasn't so lucky. The U.S. State Department doesn't give them to everyone who asks. Otherwise, more people would avoid risking their lives to cross the border. Mexicans and other immigrants come to the U.S. to escape corruption and make a better life for themselves and their families, but there is a big circle in motion. People complain about illegal Mexican immigrants, yet ignore the problem created by supporting criminals with drug deals from Mexico. If there was more open talk about the reality of the problem, there would be better awareness about it. Education on the subject is important.

When I applied for a visa the second time, I didn't get it. It was basically the same experience I had the first time with a different person behind the desk. I didn't have proof that I could afford to return to Mexico after a short visit. They weren't interested in handing out visas to immigrants who intended to leave for good. But I had to try again.

The third time I showed up at the Immigration office it was about 1 p.m. and I was last on line. When it was my turn, the man in the office acted like he had no time for me. He was one of four officers sitting in a cubicle. I could see it was getting late by the clock on the wall in front of me. The office was in the American Embassy, so they were all American.

There were green lights on the wall that flashed to indicate when it was OK to approach the desk. When I looked up and saw the green light, he motioned toward me. He wore glasses and a suit and spoke Spanish with a heavy American accent when he asked me how I was doing. The fact that he made the effort to speak to me in Spanish was comforting. Then he started looking at his watch while quickly flipping through my paperwork. When he asked why I wanted to go to the U.S., I told him I had friends to visit. When he said, *Come back for your visa at 4 p.m.* I was like, *Really? There is a God!*

The way I felt at that moment reminded me of the day I was in the car with the gun to my head. I had the same sense of tension that I had waiting for my visa and the same relief as when the criminals told us to run, especially when I went back to the office and held my visa in my hands.

At 19 years old, I was determined to get to the U.S., start a new life and discover a new world. Other than Manuel, I was the only one of 10 friends to get a visa. I didn't have the money to go, but getting the visa was the hard part. Getting the money together would be easy.

Before I had a chance to plan my trip, something happened. Bertha's uncle, whose nickname was "Monkey," came home from work one day when I was visiting and we started talking. He knew I had a visa when he said he wanted to go to the United States. He said, *I have a coyote friend* (smuggler), *who can help. He won't charge us to cross the border, but we have to pay for his bus ticket and food.*

I knew he had several other friends who wanted to go and I knew people too who wanted to go, but didn't have visas. Understand the desperation of some people who cross the border illegally. They have families and are propelled by the determination to support them, even if it means illegally escaping the poverty, crime and lack of opportunity.

Monkey wasn't one of them. He lived in one of three apartments in Bertha's house, was in his 40s and had a decent job as a welder for a big construction company, and money wasn't much of an issue for him. He wasn't rich, but he did well. But he was also a recovering alcoholic and a sponsor for other recovering alcoholics. Monkey was only looking for an adventure.

I didn't know it at the time, but a few years before I got my visa, when Ronald Reagan was president of the U.S. in the 1980s, immigration became a political focal point. Since then, immigrants (legal immigrants, too) have been associated with criminals who pose a threat to the U.S.

In 1985, President Reagan signed the Immigration Reform and Control Act, which meant it would be harder for me to cross the border than it might have been years before that. I'm not sure if knowing that would have influenced my actions, but I was young and didn't think much about the legal aspect of it.

Please don't hold this against me when eating my tacos. The idea of crossing the border was mostly about adventure and escape. I had imagined swimming across the Rio Grande and going into the desert, but that wasn't enough. I wanted to live it. I wanted to be there. I, Leo Cervantes, the one who kicked his mother like a kick boxer and slid into the world like a bar of soap, and found his way home from the market by himself at 3 years old, said, *This could be my opportunity!*

I also wanted to go with my friends support them. I thought, why should they stay in a place where crime was everywhere? They had nothing to do with the killings or the mafia. These were my good friends who needed to get out. Once I made up my mind, no one could change it, not even my mother. But even she didn't try very hard to discourage me because she had raised me to have determination. She was worried, but I assured her that because I had my visa it wasn't entirely illegal.

When I told Bertha, she said, *I can't believe you.*

I said, *You know me, right?*

And she said, *You're right. I know you and you will be fine.*

We were on a bus on our way to a town called *Ciudad Acuña*, which borders El Rio, Texas. About six of us, including a "coyote" who would be our guide, would ride the bus for two days to get to the border. I had left my home and my family, and whether it was for better or for worse was uncertain. But my mentality has always been that the only way to find out if something is going to work or not is to do it. We were going to a place where we didn't know the language. We understood there would be excitement, as well as danger, and only God could know what was coming, but we were willing to take the risk.

Before I left Mexico, I had worked with some of my friends who were plumbers. We used to have to go inside the ducts of 10-story buildings. I was on the 8th floor of one of the buildings one day when there was a crane for lifting cement on top of another nearby building. When the crane collapsed and hit the side of the building I was in, it shook and made a loud noise that scared me to death.

Even though I would normally walk very carefully down and around the ducts that ran through the middle of the building, I ran down eight floors in about five seconds. I was afraid of heights, but it didn't matter because I had to get out of there. Sometimes you have no choice but to do things you don't feel comfortable doing. The same thing was true of crossing the border. It didn't matter if there would be alligators or snakes or Immigration. My friends had to do it to get to where they wanted to go and I had to go see it for myself.

In the same spirit of adventure and excitement, we wondered if we were going to die. In a way, we were invading a country, but from our perspective, we were mostly escaping our own. We had no boots or equipment and weren't really prepared in any way because we didn't know what to prepare for. I remember sitting on the bus in silence. I was looking out the windows at sights I'd never seen, like roads lined with trees and houses, through thick fog. I had a cold feeling because I didn't really know where I was going.

Eduardo had crossed the border and had his own experience, but I didn't have the benefit or the comfort of knowing exactly what it was. Only recently, he told me he had tried crossing the border into Texas eight times in two years before he made it in. Each time, he was found by Immigration and deported. Three of those times, he almost died. Once, he and the people he was with went to sleep on the street and someone approached him with a gun. Luckily, he escaped. When he tried again two years later, he got smart and paid a *coyote* to take them through Tijuana to San Diego and get them in without getting caught.

They made it! He had also found a connection to Bradley Beach, which is how he wound up there.

Border towns tend to be ugly, dirty and unpleasant—like Tijuana and San Diego, two very active places for immigrants. People go in and out, but not a lot of people live in border towns. If you think about it, who really comes to the U.S. from Mexico besides people who have nothing? The people often don't even speak proper Spanish; they speak a dialect. I hadn't seen too many places. When I was a kid, my aunt took me to Acapulco and that was the first time I ever saw the ocean. I went to Vera Cruz once and Guanajuato, and that's about it.

When my friends and I arrived in Ciudad Acuña, I realized how much I could miss my hometown, even though it was poor. I knew I was going somewhere, though I didn't know where.

For two days, we rented an old dirty hotel room in Ciudad Acuña. In particular, the bathroom was so covered in mold that I didn't want to touch anything, especially not the shower knobs. I even showered with my sneakers on. It was the kind of hotel that only immigrants like us would tolerate. At that point, I felt like I was part of an operation. Everything was different. I didn't want to be there, but I had heard so much about the Rio Grande---many stories and songs---that I was anxious to see it.

107

In Mexico, we have songs known as *corridos*, which became popular during the Revolution---the Mexican-American War in the 1840s. *Corridos* are short histories of Mexican life set to music. These long ballads narrate the stories of Mexican people---immigrants, heroes, political leaders and those who needed a way to express themselves, since this was long before people wrote memoirs.

You can learn about the war almost entirely by listening to certain songs. The rebels who lived in the mountains wrote *corridos* about people like "Pancho" Villa, a Mexican revolutionary leader who became a folk hero (even though he was a killer and a bandit) because he was an advocate for the poor.

A lot of *corridos* I'd heard were about immigrants crossing the river. Our guide across the border was a guy from Guanajuato who used to come to the U.S., work for six months, go back to see his family, and travel back and forth.

Someone else, whose name I don't remember, would guide us once we got across. He was a 300-pound gorilla of a person. All he wanted was $5 from each of us for a total of $30 for crossing the river, which we knew wasn't going to be easy. We met the coyote and walked about a quarter of a mile through bushes toward the river. I was sneezing. I had chills and probably a fever, but I wasn't focused on being sick; I was too busy being young and stupid. What I was thinking was that one day I would enjoy looking back on this moment, and it was like a motor for the future.

Once we got to the edge of the river, I thought, *OK, so this is the famous Rio Grande.* In Mexico, we knew it as Rio Bravo. I wasn't that impressed because it didn't look rough.

Before we left town, Alfredo, who was good friends with my brother Eduardo, stopped at a liquor store to buy a small bottle of tequila to drink for medicinal purposes before crossing the river. I was both excited and worried listening to the coyote's instructions. We had to take our clothes off, wrap them up in a ball and put them on our heads, holding on to them with one hand. *With your other arm*, he said, *hold on to my arm.* He wanted the stronger people on the inside and the smaller ones on the outside.

My eyes were itchy and burning, and I felt funny about the whole deal. It was damp even before we got into the river. Dressed in underwear only, we stepped inside the freezing cold water. Nobody complained or showed how they felt because they just wanted to get through it. Quietly, to myself, I took a deep breath and counted "one, two, three" like I had done before getting on an airplane the first time and just about every time I had been nervous about doing something new or difficult.

I got into the freezing cold water and it rose quickly to my middle before I grabbed onto the coyote with my left arm and locked arms with Alfredo with my right arm. Alfredo was smaller than I, but I held his forearm tightly.

This was in April of 1988. Later, I learned about the 3,200 illegal immigrants who had died along the Texas-Mexico border between 1985 and 1994, mostly by drowning in the Rio Grande. They estimate that at least 330 people die at the border every year, not only by drowning, but because of heatstroke, dehydration, accidents and getting killed by other people.

Up to my neck in rushing water, near the middle of the river, I understood how people died. Every time I lifted my leg, it got away from me. The power of the current was strong. The big guy was holding three people on one arm and three on the other arm. I felt panicky because I was still afraid of water from childhood, terrified that I might drown. I was really too sick to be battling the river. Once we passed the middle of the river and got to the other end, which was the American side, the water level was waist high. What took about 20 minutes felt like forever.

The big guy had us climb up onto his shoulders and we all helped each other out of the water, where there was a chest-high dirt pile to climb. We threw our clothes over the dirt pile onto the other side. Before leaving us to the rest of our journey, the big guy wished us good luck, turned around and headed back. His $30 job was over. Our next challenge was to put our clothes back on our wet, dirty bodies, then walk through more bushes.

We had chosen to begin our journey at 6 o'clock because it would be nearly dark in case we needed to hide. We heard a vehicle approaching and started running, even though we didn't even know where to run. It was like being at war. We were running until we came to a big hole full of wet mud. There was nowhere else to hide, so when one guy ran and jumped into the mud, we all followed. I was so sick and getting worse because of the conditions of the situation. We stayed in the mud for about an hour. I was shaking with fever.

My friend and I, who were both sick, drank the tequila he had bought. My whole body was locked from not moving. My clothes were covered in mud. By the time we got out, it was so dark we couldn't see a thing. There was no light as we walked through the Texas desert with no food or water. At night, we made a fire to warm up. We thought it might even help the Immigration Patrol find us. We thought we were going to die.

We saw deer, snakes, coyotes, armadillos jumping, something else I'd never seen before. As we were walking we saw a herd of sheep, I said, *Let's catch one and eat it*. But we couldn't because they were so fast. I needed something to eat, so I picked leaves from the trees to chew on. We found what we thought were deer traps---buckets with big kernels of corn or some type of grain. We tasted it, but it was like biting into an uncooked bean. We started making jokes about the idea of starving, as if it couldn't happen. But all we brought with us were a couple of cans of sardines and two loaves of Wonder bread for six people. The coyote gave us the impression that it would only take a few hours to get to our destination in San Angelo, Texas. He didn't really want us to carry anything because traveling lightly would be easier. But we decided to take some food just in case. We each had a bottle or two of water and that was it. But the first day we didn't need it as much as we needed it the second day, when our journey through the desert really began.

We ached to know how much longer we had to walk, but our coyote wouldn't admit that he had lost direction and didn't know where we were. That night, we were climbing up a mountain and saw the light of the moon. Nobody was talking and we saw silhouettes of people. We were scared knowing that plenty of bad things can happen when you cross the border. Four or five silhouettes approached and we all held our breath. They were as afraid of us as we were of them. It reminds of a show I've been watching called *The Walking Dead* because everybody is afraid of everybody.

We said, *Who are you?* They said they were lost. We asked if they had any food, but they didn't. We started walking together and suddenly we were a group of 10 or 12. It was a relief to find people like us. But the next morning we decided to split up the group because we didn't have enough food to share and didn't want to waste time trying to agree upon which way to go. Our last can of sardines that we opened with a rock and a small butter knife someone brought would be our last meal.

For dessert, we took out a tube of toothpaste. We each had a fingertip of Crest to get rid of the dryness and the bad taste of fish in our mouths. It seemed like a very good idea, but it was also the only idea.

It was night and we saw a pick-up truck. One of the people in our group assumed the truck was Immigration and started screaming and running. Then we all started running as an automatic reaction. After about two minutes of running and realizing we had lost a couple of people along the way, we decided to stop and asked ourselves why we were running. My new-ish canvas sneakers were broken. Another guy sat down by a tree in the middle of the desert and took his boots off to find his feet bleeding. He said, *I'm sorry, I'm staying here.* We said, *You're crazy. We have to find someone or something.* But he said, *No, I'm done.*

We all agreed to leave him there and eventually go back to get him. We continued walking for another couple of hours and found a road in the middle of nowhere. There were no cars or people. About three hours later, our coyote said, *I know where we are!*

On the fourth day, we got up after spending the night on the grass covered in morning frost. When the frost melted we'd pick up a patch of grass and slurp the dew from it because we were so thirsty. One guy brought a sheet with him to lie down on, but that didn't stop his body from aching. We were all a mess. It's a good thing I was 19.

Everyone wanted to kill the coyote, especially Monkey, because the coyote was supposed to be guiding us. We walked up a mountain and came to a ranch in the middle of nowhere. We were so hungry and tired. All we wanted to do was to find something or somebody or be found by something or somebody, even Immigration. Eventually, we got our wish.

After seeing no one for a long time, we met some Latino workers. We told them we were hungry. They gave us a delicious pot of coffee to drink. They said their boss was sleeping. We could either wait to find out if he had work for us, or walk a few more miles to the store to buy some food. We were delirious, but after walking like maniacs, a few more miles didn't matter. It turned out to be about 15 miles or so more to the store.

Monkey was hallucinating, repeating, *I want a Coca Cola. I want a Coca Cola.* Finally, the coyote recognized where we were and knew about the store our friends were talking about 15 miles back. We bought some food with the little money we had. I wanted a banana and an Oreo cookie. Up to this point, having money wasn't an advantage because we were in the desert where money means nothing.

We waited outside in the bushes while the coyote went into the store. We were laughing with relief, thinking we had made it. He came out with two bags of food with the $100 or so that we had given him. He was pale. His face had dropped because walking behind him were two well-dressed Mexican-Americans holding guns. One of them said, *Nobody move. We're Immigration.*

I was relieved and we asked if they would let us eat first. They agreed. They were very nice guys. One said, *You're very lucky to be alive. Somebody spotted you two or three days ago. But when we couldn't find you, we thought you were dead. We have to follow the law and take you back to the border.*

I thought, this is the end of my story in Texas, as we got into their van and drove back to where we thought our friend might be. We remembered the road. We searched, but couldn't find him. We walked around where we thought we had left him, but he wasn't there. They drove us another three hours, which had taken us four days to walk, back to the border and dropped us off on the other side.

I was only half-joking when I said to my friends, *I'm going back (to Mexico). I have enough material to write my book.*

The others had no choice but to try crossing again. I felt lucky that I had a choice. We said goodbye, exchanged hugs and I, along with Monkey and two others, went back to the hotel to shower and shave because we looked like the cavemen on the Geico Insurance commercial. I even had a tick on me and had to burn it off with a match. Before we could go home, we needed clothes, which we bought before returning to Mexico City.

When I got back, I told my mother what happened. She was angry because she said if I had a visa, why the hell would I do something stupid like that? But ultimately, she understood that I wanted to experience it for myself.

Leo, age 19, at Ellis Island, NY.

A New World

I was very nervous flying for the first time. Before I stepped foot on the airplane, I did my usual countdown to prepare myself for whatever was to come. *One, two, three.* I really count like that to let go of my fear. I thought it was going to be horrible---the height, feeling the altitude, the possibility of crashing. I was sweating and talking to myself. *I can't believe I'm going to do it, but I have to do it.*

Pépe and I were in it together since we both had visas. I had a window seat and forced myself to look down. Before the plane took off, I had a lot of emotions about my Mom, my family, my hometown, while Pépe was silent and relaxed immediately, as if he'd picked up and left his country many times.

So many visions came to me, especially of my childhood–the beautiful and the horrible flashing in pictures in my head. The minute the wheels left Mexican ground, I felt disconnected from everything I knew and loved. Even now, when I go there, I'm excited. But when I leave, I always get the same feeling. I have tears in my eyes wondering when I'll be back.

Taking off itself wasn't too bad. But every time the plane moved a little bit, I braced myself, wondering how safe it was and if we were going to crash. The altitude didn't bother my stomach, but when I realized how high I was in the air, 40,000 feet or whatever it was, I got a little nervous. When I started to enjoy the view I was pretty comfortable because I had done the hardest, scariest part for me, which was boarding the plane. I had the same thoughts as when I crossed the border: *What's coming? Where am I going?*

I knew it was the beginning of a new life. I was thinking, here I go to see a new place. I had experienced a river, and now I was experiencing an airplane. There were beautiful women---the airline hostesses---talking to me in a different language. I had to answer back in Spanish, *No hablo ingles.*

When the plane took off I left my heart there. I assumed it was the end for Bertha and me. I didn't express it to her, but I felt that if life was going to put us together again, that would be fine, and if not, then it had been a pleasure. It was OK. It had to be.

Looking down, I knew Pépe and I were a lot better off than a lot of people on the ground beneath me. I thought about people who were being chased, or raped or drowning in the river trying to cross the border. And there I was, on a plane flying above it. I had perspective. My feeling was, *Thank God I'm here. I'm fine. Not everybody has the opportunities I have.*

Just like crossing the border, it wasn't good enough to hear someone else's stories about living in the U.S. I wanted to have the experience. This would be more than a vacation could offer me. It would be a chance to remove myself from things I felt were holding me back.

Six months after being picked up by Immigration, Eduardo, who was already living in the U.S., sent me $700 to buy a plane ticket. He was making money working in construction and was better off than we were in Mexico. When I got the money he sent in the mail, I started making plans by inviting Pépe to come with me. I didn't call Eduardo to warn him that we were coming because I wanted to surprise him.

His return address on the envelope said Bradley Beach. When we arrived at Newark Airport, we went to the Immigration window, where there was a person speaking to us in English, which I didn't understand, though that's not why I was staring at her. I was surprised by what she looked like because I had never seen a black person in my entire life. Then we went to Customs, where a man asked us in "broken" Spanish why we had come to the United States. We said we were there to visit a friend. He checked our passports and our luggage. He gestured for us to go away and as we exited, I could see the light. Automatic doors opened to the sounds of cars, taxis and people. I focused on putting one foot in front of the other while we walked to the taxi stand. I had the envelope from Eduardo and pointed to the Bradley Beach address for the dispatcher, who would pair us up with a driver who knew how to get there.

The second black person I would see in my life was our driver. As we jumped into his yellow taxi, Pépe and I were smiling from ear to ear, feeling like we were just born. We got on the Garden State Parkway, which to most people is just a highway that takes you to Atlantic City, New York City and some other places. To me, it was beautiful with the colors of spring. If we hadn't come from the jungle, we might not have appreciated it in the same way. I was more used to garbage and cardboard houses than I was to beautiful landscapes. Too often people don't appreciate what they have. Sometimes they are blinded, so they don't see what's right in front of them. It makes me thank God I come from where I come from.

Twenty or 30 minutes into the taxi ride we started watching the clock, wondering how much the trip was going to cost. We realized we had underestimated the distance from the airport. We had about $400 to spend on the whole trip. When the driver stopped the car, the meter said $70, but he asked us for

$100. We didn't care that much, but for a second I thought I was still in Mexico. But really, we were just happy to be there.

We knocked on the door of what we thought was Eduardo's house and a young dark kid of about 12 came to the door and said Eduardo didn't live there anymore. We gasped because we thought we were in trouble. He said, *But wait! I know where he lives and I can take you there.*

We were relieved and began dragging our wheeled luggage on what we assumed would be a short walk. He said my brother was living in a house in Asbury Park, which was about a half mile away. Driving by us was a red Cabriolet convertible with a group of beautiful blonde girls, who smiled and waved at us. I said to Pépe, *Welcome to America.*

Asbury Park reminded me of Ciudad Acuña, the border town full of transients, like a different jungle across the border. Even though it was poor, there were houses, which you don't see in poor sections of Mexico. But they were all painted same colors. In Mexico, the houses are built the same, but are painted different colors like blue, white, green and pink. The only way we could tell where we were in Asbury Park was by the names of the streets.

When we got to the house, we knocked on the door and one of Eduardo's roommates, who we later found out was Miguel "Montana," came to the door. He called for my brother. When he came to the door and he saw us, his eyes opened wide and his hands flew up to his head.

What the hell are you doing here?

We said, *Surprise!* I like to surprise people because it's important to me that people remember special moments in life. Our surprise was seeing Eduardo's new look with a bushy beard. He was almost unrecognizable to me. He was also dirty since he had just gotten home from his construction job.

As we talked in the doorway before he invited us in I could see he was not the brother I knew in Mexico---the party guy, who also dressed nicely. He was more like someone who had been kidnapped. He wasn't himself.

Finally, we were invited into the small, two-story house that looked like a homeless shelter because there were so many people inside. Eduardo said Miguel was one of 13 roommates. I knew I'd have to find my own way to survive this American jungle. My brother had a look on his face that said, *Please get me out of here.*

He asked if we were hungry. We were, so he led us down the street to a Chinese restaurant. It would be my first time trying Chinese food. On the walk there, Eduardo said, *I can't believe you guys are here.*

He was still in shock, but I know he was happy to have company. Living the way he lived was not easy. As we walked down Memorial Drive, I thought of Ciudad Acuña aing. Somehow it felt like there was a big cloud hanging over Asbury Park. We crossed the train tracks to Main Street, and arrived at the restaurant. Pépe and I were excited to hear Eduardo order food in English. We walked inside and the Chinese guy said to my brother, *Hola, amigo. Pollo con arroz?*

I couldn't believe the Chinese guy spoke Spanish. I wasn't too happy that my brother hadn't learned to speak English. After eight months, he only knew a few words. When I started trying to learn, I realized how complicated it was, but by then I already understood a lot. I just couldn't translate it all.

Back at his house, Eduardo said he was going to get *La Gorda.* We didn't know what that meant, but we knew *gorda* is the feminine tense of the word fat. When we saw her it made sense. *La Gorda,* the owner of the house where Eduardo lived, was obese. Her real name was Milagros. They only called her *La Gorda* behind her back.

My brother told us to stay outside while he went inside to talk to *La Gorda* before inviting us in. She spoke Spanish, but a funny Spanish. She was Puerto Rican. My experience with people from other countries was limited to an Argentinean guy and two guys from El Salvador who worked at the stadium back in Neza.

La Gorda looked at us up and down as if we were merchandise. She said we looked good. It was true. We were nicely dressed and she was surprised we were both legal and well put-together, unlike so many other Mexicans she knew. She invited us to stay and start paying rent as soon as we got jobs. It was a small house with about 13 people living there, although it was hard to know exactly how many since people were coming and going all the time. The kitchen was off limits; everyone had to either eat out or order in. A lot of them worked in restaurants and came home late at night.

We were introduced to one of the residents at House of *La Gorda* named Santiago from Oaxaca, who had been hit by a car. He wore a brace on his head and used a wheelchair to get around. Since he didn't have a job, I thought it was strange that he had the largest bedroom in the house with one bed in it. As the roommates trickled in, we were introduced and discovered that most of them were people my brother knew from back home in Neza. All of us were Mexican. It was like a big family. But I wondered about *La Gorda's* relationship with Santiago. She took him to doctors, found him a lawyer and got part of his settlement money for her trouble. It seemed to me like she was controlling him.

At bedtime, Pépe and I were invited to sleep in Santiago's room on the floor with five others. In the morning, everyone went to work, except for Santiago.

When I asked my brother why he was there I also had to wonder why I was there. I thought there had to be other opportunities, especially knowing that laborers were in high demand. I didn't understand why he wanted to be in a house with so many people and only one small bathroom, where we weren't able to use the kitchen, and had no TV.

La Gorda wanted to take us for a spin in her van, which did have a TV in it. It was not easy to understand her accent because she didn't pronounce every letter or even every word. On our way to Shop-Rite, she was trying to say that she thought Asbury Park was beautiful. We walked inside and she asked, *How do you like this store?* We didn't say much because we weren't that impressed. She assumed we'd never seen a nice store before this one. It didn't take long to figure out the real reason she brought us with her. She wanted us to carry the bags for her.

After living in the house for about 10 days, I found out *La Gorda* actually was, in a way, holding the people who lived in the house hostage. I understood Eduardo didn't know anybody else, but I am different. I would have done anything I had to do to avoid living in that environment. She collected $150 a month from each person, so the more people the better. Eduardo was convinced she would call Immigration on us if we left.

In less than two weeks Pépe and I got jobs at the Cypress Inn, a restaurant not too far away from the house. Someone had told us to check the place out. So we did, they handed us aprons and we got hired on the spot. We bought bicycles and traveled a couple of miles from Asbury Park to a place called Wanamassa. From the minute I got the job, I worked as though I was trying to get somewhere. I observed everyone there and quickly figured out my place.

Washington, whose job was to wash the pots and pans, was off during my first week. I hadn't met him yet and I didn't know what the situation was, but I could tell by looking at his work that there was a problem. No one asked me to do it, but I took all the stained, greasy pots and pans, and washed them until they were shiny. Pépe and I scrubbed the kitchen until we were sweating and it was spotless. Pépe was more of a follower. I was the one who said, let's do this or that, and he would do it with me. I did all kinds of extra jobs because I wanted to transform things. When Washington---a tall black guy---came back to work, I watched him go out and smoke, eat something and go back to washing dishes without saying a word. There was no happiness there.

I thought of the Cypress as a big ship and it was the chef's job to keep the ship above water, or in other words, to keep everything running smoothly. Working with Butch, the chef, was like being on the Titanic while it was sinking. Butch came in every morning at 9 or 10 a.m. and took two six-packs of beer from the bar. He drank and smoked while he prepped and kept control of the whole kitchen. While washing the dishes, I watched him cutting prime rib, grilling steaks, yelling at everyone and sweating from the heat of the broiler and the grill. It was like watching a show.

But Friday and Saturday nights were more like a storm when things weren't going right and Butch screamed orders until the situation stabilized. I watched him turn into a monster when someone made a mistake, like getting an order wrong, which meant Butch would have to make the order all over again the right way. The servers walked around with their heads and faces hanging down when he screamed at them. I always assumed they were doing something wrong. But I realized it wasn't them. Butch was very strict and crazy while he was working, then later, he was quiet. It wasn't personal for him. He had a job to do and that's all he cared about in that moment.

I was afraid of Butch even though he liked me. When I wasn't washing dishes, he called me *amigo* and shouted out orders. Instead of explaining in English, since I didn't understand, he showed me what he wanted me to do, like peel carrots or chop onions, or whatever he needed done. He moved around fast like a warrior. I was busy too, but not too busy to watch him and learn to respect him.

One day, when he noticed the difference in how much cleaner the kitchen was, he wanted to know what had happened. That's when he started to like us. There was action and something to learn, which made me happy to be there. I shined, cleaned and did everything I could to make it a better place and he noticed that and told Nick, the owner.

Butch was tough, but I didn't mind. In fact, I began to appreciate it. I wanted to make him like me. Not only that, but I didn't understand some of the other workers and their lack of pride in their jobs.

There were two managers, Bill and Leon. Leon was a tall, thin black guy not to be mistaken with Washington. Leon's tuxedo was always dirty, which looked out of place in such a fancy restaurant.

A Mexican guy named Isai came to work. I was impressed with him because he had a car, a driver's license and a green card. He spoke broken English and was able to translate for us so we understood what we needed to do. Finally, I met someone who was content. He told me he had been working there for 10 years. He was proud of the fact that he had just bought a car for $15,000. I thought that was a lot of money.

At the end of the night, we cleaned the whole floor by hosing it down. At 2 a.m. when we were finished, Pépe and I got on our bicycles and pedaled home. Washington got picked up by a taxi. Isai got in his car. *Hasta mañana.*

I remember someone I'd met before I left Mexico, while I was working with plumbers in an apartment. There was an older man about 60 years old doing tile. He was complaining that his helper didn't show up to work that day. He claimed that he had been the best helper ever, and it had taken him 20 years to learn how to be a great helper. He was proud of himself, but it made me think that I wouldn't want to be a dishwasher or a plumber's helper for 20 years or even 10 years. I had higher

131

expectations. And now, here I was in the kitchen, hearing Isai talk about being in the kitchen for 10 years.

One day the owner of the Cypress, Nick Kouvel, came in and attempted to speak to me in Spanish. He said, *Amigo, come here. Everybody says you're a good guy. I want you to make more money, so you're going to be a busboy.*

He acted like it was a good thing, but I didn't want to do it. For one thing, I didn't understand English. I was afraid someone would ask me for something and I wouldn't understand. But it didn't matter. Nick told Butch that I would be a dishwasher in the morning and a busboy at night.

On my first night, Bill, the manager, said I looked nice in my uniform---a black vest and bow tie, white shirt and black pants. There was another bus boy from Jamaica named Glen, who was going to help me learn how to do my new job. I was nervous because I didn't know what anyone expected of me. I proved it when someone knocked a knife on the floor from a big table full of people. Bill nudged me so I would see it. So what did I do? I picked up the knife and put it back on the table, which made Bill's mouth drop open and his hands fly up to his head. I guessed putting the knife back on the table was the wrong thing to do. Seated at the table was a nice, well-dressed family, who started laughing. Bill explained that I was new, but all I really wanted to do was go back and hide in the kitchen and stay there. Not being able to speak English was so embarrassing to me that I made up my mind that I was going to learn. I went to Sears in Seaview Square Mall and bought a small closed-captioned TV, which was new at the time. I started watching American shows, music videos, Pop-Up Video and other shows that helped me learn English. I also bought an English dictionary, and listened to music CDs like Madonna's *La Isla Bonita*.

In the hallway of the restaurant, there was a blackboard where my co-worker Jim tried to help me learn English by drawing pictures and words. That was a mistake because it was confusing. I felt like I was never going to learn, but I realized that you have to erase Spanish from your mind to learn English and learn the new words as if they were the only words. I was able to understand, but not put it all together.

After about a month in the U.S., I was on the lookout for another place to live. It wasn't uncommon for us to gather over a pizza at night after work and talk while we ate. The group of us from Neza agreed that we felt exiled, even though we left Neza willingly. Maybe it was that we resented the fact that the place where we grew up wasn't safe for us anymore and we weren't entirely sure we were safe yet. Everything was so new.

We would get excited when we got a raise or someone expressed appreciation for our work. We shared information about how much we were being paid and the things that happened to us while in this new world. Mexico was full of Mexicans. In Asbury Park, races were mixed.

A young black girl lived in the house next door, which was so close to ours you could almost touch it. When one of the guys in our house discovered her dancing naked in the window with the shades up one night it became a regular thing to watch her. She must have wanted an audience. I only watched her once because I wasn't especially interested.

House of *La Gorda* wasn't a terrible place to live, but I knew we could do better. Everyone was afraid of *La Gorda* calling Immigration, but Pépe and I didn't care because we had our visas. Through my brother, we met another group of Mexicans from Oaxaca. Eight of us were from Neza. We played on a soccer team and one day when we all went to play, one of the guys named Oscar mentioned that there was another house for rent. I reminded Pépe that we shouldn't be afraid of *La Gorda* since we were legal. I wanted everyone from Neza to move out of *La Gorda's* house.

Leo (right) in the kitchen at Cypress Inn with a co-worker, Ian.

The house Oscar suggested was an old four-bedroom on First Avenue that was not only ugly, but dirty with roaches. We knew we would have to clean it up. The rent was $1200 a month for all of us to split. Some of the guys thanked *La Gorda* and told her they were going to move because they needed more room. It was true. It turned out she didn't mind us leaving. In fact, she wished us good luck. Since there were only three or four people left, we were surprised she didn't get upset. It was a reminder that the things we waste time worrying about usually don't happen.

My brother worked for two guys, Jimmy and Donald, in construction. I found out about one of their friends they called Eggy, a teacher who wanted to have a landscaping business in the summer. Since the Cypress was a night job, I had nothing to do in the morning.

My first day of work with Eggy started at 7 a.m. When he picked me up in his van, he started talking to me in English. It was frustrating that every time I said, *No ingles,* he kept talking. He turned the radio on and seemed to be commenting about whatever was being said. But I didn't understand any of it.

Eventually, we arrived at a big beautiful house. We took the machines out and he showed me how to use the machines to mow the lawn. We went to three houses that day. One of them had a swimming pool and a beautiful dark blonde 20-something-year-old who lived there and liked to swim and sunbathe in her bikini. I looked at her thinking I could have someone like her one day and a big house like that with a pool.

By noon, I was ridiculously hungry, dripping with sweat and tired. We had been working really hard. But he kept working until 1 p.m., and by then, I was really feeling it. He finally said, *Amigo, lunch!*

We got back in the van and pulled into a place that looked like a tavern. We sat down and looked at the menu. I handed it back to him because I couldn't read it. He ordered two beers. I was 19, and I didn't know it was legal for me to drink. When the waitress brought us two cold, sparkling beers, I drank it. I didn't love beer, but it was refreshing. While waiting for our food, we ate the bowl of popcorn on the table. Then she brought a plate with half a barbecued chicken, coleslaw and chips. I was excited until she put the plate in front of Eggy.

There was another plate with a big sandwich on it, potato chips and a pickle. I had never tasted a pickle. I was in a different world with different cuisine. He said something else that I didn't understand, but I was thinking, *You don't have to tell me what to do.* I took a bite of my sandwich and stopped. So many things came to mind. I was very hungry, but I thought I had

137

been served rotten meat. I thought of the dead dogs at the garbage dump in Neza while Eggy was very excitedly eating his chicken. I wasn't sure what to do. I couldn't figure out how to tell this guy that my food was possibly poisonous. The funny thing was that it smelled really good, but tasted rotten. I wanted to spit it into a napkin. It tasted like vinegar. So I ate a chip and drank some more beer and swallowed the whole mouthful. I didn't want to make him feel bad. I took another bite, a chip and a beer. I took a bite of the pickle and didn't like that either.

We finished eating and went back to work at another house. At 4:25, we stopped and he said, *Cypress Inn*. When he dropped me off, he said, *See you mañana*. I went inside the restaurant and the first thing I did was make a tuna sandwich with *jalapeños*, still trying to erase the taste of my rotten sandwich.

At 3 a.m., in the shower, then in bed, I thought about my day, my past, my future, my present. I was sleeping on the floor, but at least there was no *La Gorda*. It was just Miguel (the guy who had first opened the door when I arrived at *La Gorda's*). I was happy we had more space and two bathrooms.

Bright and early at 7 a.m., Eggy knocked on the door. I jumped in the van, and just like the first time, he spoke English as if I understood. But I didn't mind. I smiled at him because I knew he was a good guy.

At lunchtime, I tried to tell him yesterday's lunch was not good. It was very frustrating that he couldn't understand me. I was even more frustrated when we showed up at the same place, sat at the same table and had popcorn and beer again. I have always been one to take the positive out of the negative. Always. From day one. But I was feeling a little bit negative as I was about to find out if my lunch was rotten the day before. I smelled it and it smelled the same, which made me sure it would taste the same, and it did. I guessed that was how it was supposed to taste, so I ate it to fill my stomach. I was happy to have food, no matter what it was.

Day number three. Eggy came to get me at 7 a.m. We worked until 1 p.m., when he said, *Amigo, lunch!* But this time, I said, *No lunch!* To his surprise, I handed him a sandwich that I had made for us at the restaurant. I was happy because he liked it.

After working one week, he invited me to come over and help paint his house. He told my brother that because I was such a good worker, he wished I had a driver's license and could do the landscaping jobs myself. He treated me like gold.

Years later, I decided to try pastrami and mustard for what I thought was the first time. But I recognized it immediately as what I thought was a rotten sandwich. I grew to like it because I got used to it. It goes to show you how you can adjust your mind into believing something is either rotten or delicious.

At the DMV in Asbury, using our visas that would eventually expire, we were able to apply for a driver's license. When we took the test in Spanish, we were the only ones in our group to have visas. Jimmy, Eduardo's ex-boss in construction, sold us a Le Car for $375 and it lasted about six months.

Asbury Park still felt weird to me partly because I didn't like where we lived on First Avenue. One night, a friend of ours stopped at the liquor store to buy some beer because someone else was bringing pizza. I was inside the house when all of a sudden my friend flew through the door screaming, "Help me. Help me!"

I left Mexico to escape violence only to find more violence in Asbury Park. It was the Puerto Ricans against the Mexicans. My friend was approached by a group of Puerto Ricans, who stopped him in the street because they either wanted his money or the beer he was bringing to our house. As he was telling us the story, we could hear them yelling obscenities outside. They wanted to kick our asses. Then they threw some rocks at the windows and broke a few of them. They were mad because my friend wouldn't give them anything. Eventually they left because they knew someone would call the cops on them.

My experience with people from other countries had been limited because not too many people from other countries had any reason to visit Neza. Here, I was Mexican, but called Latino. I was surprised by the diversity and the segregation. I wondered, *Is that how it goes here?*

We used to work with Jimmy and Donald to help them paint another house they owned on Fifth Avenue near Wanamassa. While we were there we used to imagine living on that side of Asbury Park. We thought it must be expensive.

A few months later, they asked us if we wanted to rent an apartment in the house. So Pépe, Eduardo and I left the other group and moved in. Both the house and neighborhood were nicer than the First Avenue house. I could finally breathe.

Working at Cypress exposed me to so many things. I learned that someone could be good at something and not be happy doing it. I was happy being a dishwasher and mopping the floor and carrying boxes, not because I loved doing those things, but because I was happy to have a job. While I was working and sweating, I'd remember my Mom calling it exercise.

Nick always spoke beautifully of me and appreciated the work I did there. When I did something good, which was really just doing my job, he would use me as an example. In a way, I hated it, but it was definitely better than the kind of attention I got in school for not turning in my homework. I just wanted to do my thing; I didn't need recognition.

Even though I was a busboy didn't mean I was too busy to help the dishwasher if he needed me, or that I wouldn't clean the walls if they were dirty. I gladly did the work other people wouldn't do. I didn't realize at the time that I was acting like a restaurant owner, but Butch appreciated it. One day he took a big piece of prime rib from the grill and some potatoes, put it on a plate and handed it to me. He said, *You are the hardest-working guy in the place. I like you.*

Here was a hard-working monster chef who worked from 9 in the morning to 9 at night calling me the hardest-working guy in the place. For me, it was like coming home from the war and receiving a medal. He never even stopped for lunch himself. He ate sandwiches while he worked. Although he was nice to me, he was sour because he was divorced and had a couple of kids. Now I can understand the pressure he was under at work, and the fact that going home wasn't fun made him miserable. He smoked, drank and didn't say much to anyone. But I started seeing a nicer person in him when he met Debbie, one of the waitresses. Debbie was a beautiful, sweet lady. He used to tell her how much he liked me and the way I worked. That year they invited Pépe and me to celebrate Christmas with them. I asked them if Eduardo could come too and they welcomed him too.

In 1991, I went back to Mexico to visit because I missed my Mom and my family. I never thought about returning other than to visit because I was doing well here. I spent less than two weeks in Neza, and then returned to continue my new life.

In 1992, Pépe moved out, returned to Mexico and never came back. Eduardo met a girl named Lorena, who moved in with us. Lorena didn't work, which didn't bother me until one night when I came home from work to find cups and glasses on my bed. I thought it was weird, but I didn't think much of it other than to take them down to the kitchen and put them in the sink before going to sleep. I asked Eduardo about it the next day. He said, *When you dirty something, you have to clean it yourself because Lorena is not our maid.*

I didn't say anything, but she was living there without paying rent. I didn't expect her to clean up after me, but to get upset about a few cups and glasses didn't make sense. I'm easygoing, so I didn't make a big deal out of it. And it's a good thing because he married Lorena and is still with her to this day. Instead, I told Luis, who worked at the Cypress with me, that I wanted to move out. He was a happy, funny guy from Neza, who had no plans or direction, but I liked him anyway. I didn't know him at the time, but it turned out that he lived less than a mile away from my house when we were growing up. Now he needed a new place to live, too. We found a beautiful apartment in Neptune and I moved without ever explaining to Eduardo. I didn't want to create a problem.

I suspect that part of the reason Luis lacked motivation was because he smoked a lot of marijuana. One day, he asked me if I minded if he smoked. I said, *It's no good for you.* But of course, he did it anyway, and I sat and watched him. I had never tried it before because I had been turned off by all illegal drugs while living in the jungle of Mexico, where innocent people died so that other people could get high. It didn't make sense to me and I didn't understand why anyone would want to do it. Watching Luis as his eyes got all bloodshot didn't convince me that it was fun, but since I had never tried it before and he asked me to try it, I did. After three hits, I said, *Look at you. You look like an idiot.* I probably looked like an idiot, too.

Luis liked the band Scorpions, so he put on a VHS tape for us to watch. He said, *Just relax.*

After about 10 minutes went by while we were watching the band, I realized I heard nothing but the guitar. No drums or voice. I saw the singer moving his mouth, but I didn't hear sound. Suddenly, I was sweating. I had to run to the bathroom, where I threw up a few times. After that, I took a shower. I promised myself I would never smoke marijuana or touch drugs ever again. I needed to keep my mind as clear as possible, especially when it came to learning English, which I believed was important to my success. By then, my English vocabulary was about 50 percent there.

I remember the day my knowledge of English was tested. It was another situation that required me to count to three. Nick told Butch that someone had to make a delivery to Jersey Shore Medical Center in Neptune. Since they didn't have an official delivery person, Nick asked if I could do it. There was a party going on there and they had ordered a few platters of food. I didn't feel entirely sure that I could do it, but saying no to challenges wasn't my style.

The test began when Butch made me talk to the person who called from the hospital to give me specific instructions about where to make the delivery. I was so nervous, but I listened carefully to the instructions. I was terrified, but once the food was in my car, I had no choice but to do it. As I was driving, I imagined the directions I needed to follow and I realized how much English I actually understood and how vivid my imagination was and still is. It felt good to be able to do what was expected of me.

Less than a year later, I got a call from Bertha. We hadn't had much contact since I left and I was surprised to hear from her.

She said, *Guess what? I applied for my visa and I got it! Is it OK if I come visit you?*

As I said yes, I knew my life was about to change again. A month later, she came and I rented a car to pick her up. I didn't have directions to JFK Airport and I only knew that I should head north. I still don't know how I got there, but somehow even without a GPS system to guide me, I found it and brought her to my apartment.

I was happy for her to come here and start a new life. I was also happy I could help her. We lived together for about six months and everything was good until she got homesick. She would talk about her family and how much she missed them. I felt bad, so I encouraged her to go back home.

After about two months when she called, she started saying how much she missed me. It was a problem for her. So, we decided she should come back so we could try again. When she returned a couple of months later, I suggested she go to school while I worked to pay the bills. Then, when she would become something, it would be my turn to open a business. But she didn't have the same motivation.

When she first came to New Jersey, she got a job working in a plastic factory, and that was OK with her. But her real happiness was taking care of the house. Although we weren't married, Bertha was the perfect housewife. She was a great cook and kept an immaculate, organized house decorated with flowers in almost every room. Everything smelled good and looked good and was in its proper place. And she sang while she worked. There was not even a hint of dust on any surface. Ever. The refrigerator was even perfectly organized. The bathroom was beautiful, always smelled nice, with flowers and monogrammed towels. Our clothing was always ironed and folded perfectly in drawers. I was afraid to dirty anything because it looked so nice.

She was also creative. She could make pictures out of beans and noodles. But a housewife was all she wanted to be. We moved back to Fifth Avenue near the lake in Asbury Park, not far from Jimmy and Donald's house, to try and make it work.

Between 1993 and 1994, the Gulf War was still in progress and there was a recession. That meant business for white-tablecloth restaurants went downhill. People either didn't have the money to spend on dining out or didn't want to spend it and Cypress Inn was a victim of that situation.

John Kuwati, the manager, who had left a nearby restaurant called the Shadowbrook to manage Cypress, said to me, *Leo, you're a good guy. You should work at the Shadowbrook. Andre, the chef, would love you.* He offered to introduce me to Andre, a 55-year-old Puerto Rican guy who spoke Spanish. He asked if I was looking for a job. I needed a new job, but Cypress was my home. I loved everybody and everybody loved me and I was so comfortable there. I was hoping it wasn't going to close. I thought maybe we'd get lucky and things would pick up again.

One day, I went in to work and Nick was talking to some people sitting at the bar. I felt so down ever since John had said things did not look good for the restaurant. I wasn't even paying attention to what Nick was talking to the people about. Once again, I wondered where the wind was taking me. I had worked there for four years. The last week before it closed, we didn't even get paid because there was no money.

After about a week of not working, I called Andre. He said I should show up on Friday, and be prepared to work. When I got to the Shadowbrook, Andre introduced me to everybody and showed me around. There were two kitchens divided by one wall, one for parties and banquets, and the other for *a la carte* dining. He introduced me to Nick, the head *a la carte* chef.

Andre said, *Nick, this is Leo. He's going to help you here tonight.*

Then he said to me, *Whatever you need let me know. Waiters are going to come and give you orders and you're going to cook.*

They hadn't been busy for a long time because business had been bad for the same reason the Cypress shut down. In fact, they were going to shut down *a la carte* dining at the Shadowbrook. Andre explained this to me 10 minutes before starting the show. I guess that was my lucky night because we got hit hard with business. There were tickets and more tickets coming in and I didn't even know the whole menu yet.

Nick was being kind of miserable. His mouth was crooked and I could feel his negative energy. I went crazy that night. Cooking for the 100 or so people who came in for dinner meant that we were moving around like we were at war again. Between the two of us, there was a lot to do.

I didn't know it, but Nick was extra miserable because he knew they were trying to get rid of him. He was sour and unfriendly because he was afraid of losing his job to me. So when I asked for help with details about how to put certain dishes together, his answer was, *I don't know. I didn't hire you. Ask Andre.*

I didn't like that he wasn't willing to work together. He was trying to sabotage me so I wouldn't do a good job. But at the end of the night, Andre and a couple of other guys told me I had done a great job. They were excited about how busy we were. I appreciated it, but I had to decline. I couldn't take the job. I said, *I'm sorry, but this is not for me.*

I told him I couldn't work alongside someone who wasn't happy to be there. Andre said, *I'm going to tell you the truth. We need to get rid of this guy and we are looking for the right person. I think you are it. Please come back tomorrow.*

I needed the job, so I went back in the following night. Now that I knew what I knew, which was only a little bit more than I knew before, I didn't talk to Nick that much and focused on taking the orders. It wasn't like me not to laugh and have fun, even while I was trying to keep the ship from sinking, but I chose to be more serious like him.

Again, at the end of the night, Andre said, *You proved to me that you are the guy we need here on Saturdays. You don't know the menu and you had to deal with this guy for two nights, and you still did a beautiful job. Meat is difficult to get right whether it's rare or medium or well-done. Nobody sent anything back in two days. Do you know what that means? It means we need you here. I promise you, when you come in tomorrow you won't have to deal with Nick.*

I felt bad about it, but he said I shouldn't. He said, *Does he seem like he's here because he wants to work? He doesn't want to work. He's miserable, and believe me, if he had a different attitude, I wouldn't be talking to you.*

On Sunday, I parked my car in the lot and as I was walking in, Nick was walking out. That meant he went to work and got fired. He looked at me and kept going. The reason they fired him that day was because I told Andre that I would love to work there, but not with him there. I didn't think they were really going to get rid of him, but that's what they did.

The Shadowbrook was a different animal. The Cypress was all American people---the chef, the workers, the waitresses--- everybody was American. I was the only Latino. At the Shadowbrook, everyone was Latino. It wasn't necessarily better, but it was different.

After my experience at the Cypress Inn of watching Butch---the captain of the kitchen---life was giving me the opportunity to be like him in my own environment, in my own language with my own people. It was mostly Colombians. I was the only Mexican. I realized this is what happens with immigrants in a new world.

You form groups of your own people as you meet them along the way.

The banquet chef was Puerto Rican and I became the *a la carte* chef. Working *a la carte* gave me the freedom to create recipes unlike the banquet menu at the Cypress, which was always the same. I enjoyed creating soup recipes. I came up with a creamy potato soup with chorizo and dill that Robert Zweben, the owner of the Shadowbrook, especially liked. I also made scalloped potatoes and other things that weren't ordinarily on the menu.

The Shadowbrook is where I found out what it was like to be recognized. It made me feel like I was doing the right thing. Robert came into the kitchen one day holding a newspaper containing a beautiful restaurant review in The Asbury Park Press---the biggest newspaper in the area at the time---describing the food as fresh, well presented and delicious. Robert was very happy to be able to revive the *a la carte* aspect of the business. He shook my hand and said, *Thank you very much.*

I was appreciated and I wanted more of that. Now, what I'm about to tell you requires me to change some names to protect certain people who weren't thinking about the future when they did certain things. I'm also having some fun with it because it would be unlike me not to.

My friend Freakardo (obviously not his real name) from Peru was a maintenance guy at the Shadowbrook, who knew all about food and cooking. He also wanted to have his own restaurant. He would complement the way I cooked and remind me how much the Shadowbrook relied on me for the success of their *a la carte* business. When the review confirmed that, he said, *See, he needs you.*

In the beginning, cooking was hard work. But once I got good at it, it didn't feel like work anymore. The kitchen is where I get creative and satisfy my taste for good food. It's where I forget about everything, including the Freakardos of the world.

Eduardo (left) and Lorena (standing), with Berta (seated) and Leo (right) at Eduardo's apartment in Sea Bright.

My Own *Novela*

A *novela* in Spanish is a daytime drama. My favorite one on TV lately is "True Love" with Erika Buenfil, a story about how differently the rich and the poor deal with the problems in Mexico. The main character is a rich woman who falls in love with her bodyguard. I enjoy watching drama on TV better than I like dealing with it in real life. But I have to admit, each crazy thing that has happened has taught me something.

On Mondays the Shadowbrook was closed, which meant my friends from the restaurant and I had a free day to play on an indoor soccer team at a health club near the Long Branch train station. It brought me back to childhood when soccer was my sport and I was really good at playing defense. Even then I recognized it as a discipline and knew it was good exercise for my body and mind. As an adult, it became one of my favorite ways to decompress.

Another way I got rid of stress---when I wasn't driving my 1995 gold Mitsubishi Eclipse, which I loved---was driving a Ninja motorcycle, often to work. During most of my work day I stood in the kitchen in a small space, so the forward motion of the motorcycle gave me the feelings of freedom and power that I needed. I enjoyed working because I was grateful to have a job, although it was stressful. Other concerns, like my status, made being on my bike and soccer nights very important for my mental health.

Several of us had the same status issues. I was very interested to hear about an Ecuadoran lady named Maria, who worked for Immigration and was helping people become U.S. residents. It was understood that being a resident wasn't as good as becoming a U.S. citizen, but at least we would have the ability to visit our families in Mexico, and return whenever we wanted. With our current status, we were only allowed to stay for six months at a time. Before fingerprints were used for tracking, we could stay in the U.S. for a whole year without any problem. When the government cracked down on immigration, there was an advantage to traveling to and from the U.S. by car because there would be no way to get the stamp on your passport that you get when you go through Customs at the airport. If you traveled by plane and they asked to see your stamp, you could just say you had driven to Mexico.

I went back home twice while I worked at Cypress Inn because I missed my family. But the idea of returning for good was out of the question. Not only was my American journey still in progress, but I had found something I really enjoyed doing. The rush of working in the kitchen was still new, and it felt like my life had just begun.

The desire to stay in the U.S. pushed me, my brother Eduardo, and my friend Chucho, also from Neza, to visit Maria at the Immigration office in Palisades Park. We listened carefully as she explained the new program that had been very successful helping immigrants obtain their papers. In return for entering us into this program she would need our passports, birth certificates and a $750 processing fee from each of us. It was a lot of money, but at the same time it was a small price to pay for freedom.

We were so excited by the thought of being able to stay in the U.S. to work and travel back and forth to Mexico to see our families. Our lives were going to be beautiful. I was also happy because I had gotten my driver's license. It was a relief not to worry about driving illegally.

Several months later, even though we had filed out all the papers and paid Maria, we still hadn't received our working permits. We weren't sure what to think until one day in the kitchen at the Shadowbrook when I heard the Spanish radio station's breaking news about a recent bust by the FBI. It was

Maria from Palisades Park, who was not an employee of Immigration, but a criminal. She had tricked 3,000 people into thinking she was applying for their residency. She was able to get real working permits for some of her victims, but what she was actually doing was taking their money, like she took ours, and filing for political asylum without telling any of us we'd eventually have to go to court to defend ourselves. If the judge decided there was a good reason for you to stay in this country, you would keep your refugee status with a working permit. If you didn't show up, you would be on the wanted list for deportation.

Most people were very happy to get their working permits, but they never knew the truth about how the permit was obtained. When Maria's victims started getting deported and complaining about it, there was an investigation that proved her to be a criminal.

I was furious---we all were---knowing we would soon be in trouble. Instead of waiting around for something bad to happen, we decided we had to do something, though we weren't sure exactly what to do.

When I told Robert Zweben about my problem, he said, *I can't lose you.* He found a lawyer and I hired him to represent me. He suggested the Shadowbrook sponsor me so I could get a working permit. A representative from Immigration met us at the restaurant to interview Robert and me. I was so happy because he assured me I was going to be fine. I liked the Shadowbrook and was grateful to Robert for agreeing to sponsor me so I could avoid getting deported.

During the same time, Freakardo was the devil on my shoulder trying to push me to start our own business, which would mean betraying Robert. Of course, Freakardo, who seemed to have an answer for everything, suggested I ask Robert for one month off to go back to Mexico for a visit. If our business didn't work, I could go back to work at the Shadowbrook.

To make it even more attractive, he had an American friend named Freaknise (obviously not her real name), who was willing to marry me so I could get my papers, which meant I wouldn't need the Shadowbrook as my sponsor if it came to that. Since Freakardo didn't spell it out, I didn't realize at the time that part of his motivation could be to punish Robert and hurt the Shadowbrook by giving me a reason to leave.

He said, *You have to decide whether you want to work for someone else or become your own boss. We can do it!*

I thought this could be my shot. He was enticing me with my own dream. In the meantime, Robert was being so good to me.

How could I turn on him? Finally, I asked for a leave of absence so I could go to Mexico to see my family. He agreed to let me go under the condition that I find a replacement for the month I'd be away. I found a friend who was willing to fill in so I could go follow my dream with a little less guilt.

Freakardo had worked at the Shadowbrook for about 17 years, but ended his career there over something I thought was stupid. He was having trouble with Marcos, a Chilean guy, who also worked in maintenance. They were friends who often disagreed about how things should be done. Freakardo didn't usually bend because he had his own ideas and was afraid Marcos would take over his job. One day Freakardo told Robert he didn't like Marcos anymore. Robert said, *He's a good guy. He does a good job. I'm not going to fire somebody just because you don't like him.*

But Freakardo threatened to leave if Robert didn't fire Marcos, and that's just what he did. The following Monday when I went to play soccer, Freakardo told me he had quit. I was shocked because I thought it was just a threat. Even so, because we had known each other for about two years and I had nothing to do with his situation with Marcos and Robert, I let it go without passing judgment.

Our business was born when we rented the empty store behind our friend Andre's jewelry store, not far from the health club, to have parties after our soccer games. Even though it had no kitchen, we were able to put some simple but delicious meals together without doing much cooking. We would charge between $10 and $15 per person to eat, drink and socialize. Freakardo collected the money we made with the intention of saving it to eventually build a kitchen and open a real restaurant. I was very excited by that thought and knew we could do it if we stuck with it.

After eating, we'd dance, play ping-pong and the musicians in the group entertained. It was a party and we were the hosts. I was happy to have become part of the Latino population with people from all over the place.

I was having fun and couldn't grasp why Bertha wasn't happy, too. She worked as a housekeeper at The Breakers Hotel in Spring Lake. That was her thing; she was very organized. But she wasn't having any fun. Part of the problem, in my opinion, was that she would not embrace the English language or culture and struggled with displacement. She would always say she had to go back to Mexico because she missed her family. Now I know why it wasn't easy for her. But at the time, because I did not want to go back, I saw only one way to move forward and that was for us to team up and make our future happen. But Bertha would cry and when I didn't understand, I'd say, *I want to help you and grow with you. What's wrong with that?*

She tried to open up to me so many times about things, but she was never really able to. Finally I said, *OK, if I'm not your family, go back to your family.* That hurt me. That's why I told her we were done. I still wanted to be friends, but I had to separate from her. The day she was to leave, I brought her to the airport and we hugged and wished each other good luck. I was sad, but I knew it was the right thing.

I didn't want to waste time moving on, so I moved out of the apartment we had shared and accepted the invitation from Freaknise to move in with her. She was tall, thin and cute, but not an especially pretty girl, hired as a Shadowbrook hostess. Her long black hair and dark complexion made people mistake her Puerto Rican background for Italian. She was about four or five years older than I, but we were alike in some ways. She was a people person, the type who could talk to anybody. She could manipulate and portray herself however she needed to. I liked her, but the only reason I was excited about moving in with her was because I didn't want any more trouble with Immigration. She behaved just like Freakardo---feeding me what I wanted to hear about everything, including opening the business, being myself and growing as a person.

I was trying to understand Freaknise just like I had tried to understand Bertha. Freaknise was smart enough to have been a lawyer or some other kind of professional, but instead she had been a go-go dancer before getting the job as hostess. But it didn't matter to me because I accepted her as she was. Just as I needed someone to believe in me, she needed me to believe in her and I needed to help her believe in herself. It didn't take long for me to realize she was stuck.

One day she took me to a bar where she used to work and introduced me to one of her girlfriends. Because this friend of hers had been into drugs it made me sad. She had a beautiful body, but that's all she was using to move herself forward. She seemed empty and lost, which made me wonder if Freaknise had also been a drug user.

For three months we lived together and it made me uncomfortable to be with someone I didn't know very well. Part of me knew I wasn't doing the right thing. She was divorced and had a three-year-old son who didn't live with her, which made her life a little crazy dealing with her ex-. I always felt out of place, but I was also distracted enough to stay to see what would happen next.

She was very sexual and seemed to enjoy the fact that I was shy and in an experimental stage in my life. I let her seduce me into living in the moment. She made me believe her desire to help me was coming from the right place. Since she offered help at the right moment, I was willing to accept that help. It was that simple for me. But of course, there were complications.

We were going somewhere in the car one day when her ex-husband passed us in his car with their son in the back seat. When she saw them, she said, *Oh my God,* and hid her face. But he saw her and starting shouting out the car window, begging her to talk to him, but she had no interest. Her attitude was, *Get out of here.* She didn't want to talk to him at all. Then he yelled to me by name, which I was surprised he knew, *She's going to do the same thing to you that she did to me. This is your chance to disappear.*

I felt sorrier for their little boy than for either of them. I wasn't especially interested in having a long-term relationship with Freaknise. My goals were to become a resident and get my restaurant business in motion, which Freakardo kept telling me was going to happen as soon as we had enough money. In the meantime, we kept on entertaining the soccer club and saving our earnings.

Freakardo had gone home to Peru again for a short visit, most likely to visit his family, because he said something had come up. When he returned, he wasn't treating me like the friend I thought he was. He was cold and I could tell something was wrong. The day his two young daughters came with him to the club, he cornered me and caught me by surprise. Right in front of them he said, *Do you think I haven't noticed the way you look at my wife? I've seen you looking at her. I know you like her.*

The younger daughter, who was no older than 7, got upset by her father's aggression and started crying. I was shocked. His wife was definitely beautiful, but I had never looked at her at all and especially not the way he was implying. He seemed pretty serious, but I asked, *Are you joking? Because if you are, you better stop because look at your daughter.*

He said, *I'm not kidding.*

I said, *I don't know what you're talking about. You should think about what you're saying.*

I walked away with a headache not knowing what had happened to my friend. The next day when I went to talk to him, the door of our place was locked. Freakardo had the only key. Andre was at the jewelry store and said he didn't know where Freakardo could be. He told me that when Freakardo visited Peru, he consulted *la bruha* (a witch or fortune teller), who told him to beware of someone very close to him who was trying to steal his wife. I trusted Andre as Freakardo's best friend and believed he was speaking the truth. He also said that *la bruha* had warned him about someone who was going to steal his job at the Shadowbrook. That explained his issue with Marcos.

Suddenly, I felt worried about everything, but my main concern was my friendship with him, and I couldn't imagine what would become of our plans. After showing up at the club day after day and not being able to get a hold of him, I didn't know what to think other than he was gone and wouldn't be back. He had all the money we had made and left me with nothing but the bills, which I had to pay out of my own pocket. It was only a few thousand dollars, but it might as well have been a million dollars because it was money I couldn't afford to lose. The headache didn't end there.

My friend Jordi, who was also a friend of my brother, called me sounding very upset. I had introduced them to Freaknise and they had become friends. He and his wife were expecting a baby. Jordi said his wife was crying because Freaknise said she wanted my car. I didn't understand. She threatened to call

Immigration on Jordi if I didn't give her my car. I had no idea why she would do that or even threaten to do that. Nothing bad had happened between us. I hadn't even talked to her about Freakardo's accusation of me trying to steal his wife, or his disappearance. I was completely baffled.

Jordi said, *You introduced us to this woman. If something happens to my wife and baby, I'll kill her first, then you.*

Now my head was spinning and I knew I had to talk to Freaknise right away, so I went to our apartment. I said, *Would you please explain what the hell is happening?*

She said, *I need you to give me your car. I need a car and I want you to sign the title over to me. And if you don't, you'll be sorry.*

First, tell me what is going on, I insisted.

Even angrier, she said, *If you don't do it, I'm going to call Immigration on your friends and you. I'm going to get rid of all you Mexicans.*

I thought I must be dreaming. But without hesitating I went into my briefcase and gave her the title to my gold Mitsubishi, which I both loved and needed to get around.

I said, *I don't know what's wrong with you. I don't know what you're doing or why you're doing it, but if that's all you want from me, here! Have it! You could have asked me for the car and I would have given it to you without the threats.*

I know it sounds crazy, but it was true. I would have done that for her because I thought we were supposed to be helping each other. Shortly after that, I left the apartment with all my things and never went back. Suddenly, I had no job and no prospect for opening my own business. I felt ashamed about going back to the Shadowbrook, but I needed Robert to know I was available to work. When I went to talk to him he said he knew I had been working with Freakardo and wasn't happy about it. He said, *I don't need you.* I felt bad, but at the same time I understood. Before I left he said, *If I need you, I will call you.*

Now I had no money, no job, no car, no place to live, no papers, no food and fewer friends because Freaknise had called everyone we both knew and turned them against me.

I stayed with my brother Eduardo for a few days, then I went to Neptune to stay with other friends, until they became afraid of Freaknise showing up and causing trouble. Filipe, one of the guys who lived in Neptune, had a pick-up truck because he worked in construction. His flatbed with an old mattress on it became my bedroom for four or five nights. Luckily, it was summertime, and while it was good to have a place to sleep, I was down. So down, in fact, that I made the mistake of asking the question, *What else can happen to me?*

The answer was chicken pox. I was so stressed out and so depleted that I got sick. My friends invited me back to the house to sleep on their couch while I nursed a fever and tried not to scratch myself. Not only was I physically sick, but I suffered from betrayal. My mind was infected. I dug into my memory to try to figure out why this was happening to me.

Soon after that, and without any warning, Bertha came to find me sick and desperate. But I didn't want to cry on her shoulder. In my mind, we were completely over, and I didn't like the fact that she was looking down at me rather than up to me.

She expected to find Leo the go-getter, the one pushing her to succeed and strive. Instead, she found the destroyed version of me. Somehow, it gave her confidence and strength to want to lift me out of my funk. It wasn't easy. Every day I was down. I was so angry. Part of me wanted to suffer. I also didn't believe Bertha could help me without having a motive. So I said I could only accept her help if there wasn't something else behind it.

She said, *I want to help you,* and wouldn't take no for an answer. She had an apartment in Asbury Park. Eventually, she and my brother gave me money to buy a car. I will always be grateful to them for that. But again, I had to be honest and tell her that since we couldn't make each other happy, I thought we should be apart.

I received a letter from Immigration court saying I would have a hearing about my status since the Shadowbrook was no longer my sponsor. When the day came, I dressed in a suit and carried a briefcase to look as professional as possible since I had to be my own lawyer. In fact, on my way into the courtroom, a woman who appeared to be desperate to find one, asked if I was a lawyer. *I wish I was a lawyer,* I said.

When I walked into the room a beautiful blonde-haired woman was sitting at her desk with a sign: "Translator." Shortly after finding a place to sit, the judge asked who among us had a lawyer. There were only a few, and they would go first. Next he wanted to know, *Who's here without a lawyer and doesn't need a translator?*

I turned my head to look at the crowd of about 100 people and I knew I didn't want to wait for them to call out my name. My English wasn't perfect, but I knew if I opted for a translator I might be there all day with all the other 99 people who also needed one. Instead, I took a deep breath, counted to three and raised my hand.

Then he asked, *Who's here without a lawyer and needs a translator?*

Everyone else raised their hands.

When I was called on, I walked up to the judge and said something like, *Good afternoon. My name is Leonel Cervantes. I wish I had a different story to tell you.*

After hearing my case, the judge said, *You only have two options. If you leave the country voluntarily and eventually decide to return to the U.S., you won't have a negative record. If you wait to be deported, your airfare will be covered, but you will have a negative record.*

He looked at me for a minute and motioned for me to come closer to the bench, then turned off the recording device. In a quieter voice, he said, *I can tell you're a good person. You're also honest and brave. I like the way you're handling your case. We need more people like you in this country. But your country also needs more people like you. Go to back Mexico, see what you can do there, and if it doesn't work, come back, marry an American girl, fix your status and continue following your dreams.*

I thought maybe going back to Mexico would be a good thing and give me a chance to breathe deeper for a little while.

The judge put the recording device back on and asked me what I would do. I agreed to go back home. He asked how much time I needed to be ready to leave. Since it didn't matter, he gave me the maximum 90 days. After signing an agreement stating I would go back, he wished me well and sent me on way. I thanked him. As I headed toward the door I experienced such a sense of relief. I felt free because I would be legal for the next three months. On the way out, the pretty translator dressed in a gray suit sitting near the door spoke to me. *Senor Cervantes, excuse me. May I have your phone number?*

I could tell from her accent and unique way of singing her words (a little bit like Italian), she was from Argentina.

I asked, *Don't you have my phone number? I thought you already had my information.*

I assumed the court must know how to contact me since I had received the letter about my hearing.

The court has it, but I would also like to have it, she said. I asked why. She said, *In case we have to get in touch with you.*

I didn't understand.

Please let me have it. Her eyes said, *Trust me.*

This time she had me thinking it must be my lucky day. Could she be the girl to help me fix my status? I still didn't know exactly why I trusted her, but I gave her my number and she said she would call me.

In the meantime, I thought about it a lot, wondering what was going to happen. I spent days with my head spinning thinking of every single possibility. When she called a few days later, the sound of her voice made me feel instantly hopeful like something big was coming. I asked why she was calling me.

I'm calling you to ask if we can meet somewhere because I don't want to tell you this over the phone, she said.

My anxiety went through the roof. I got very nervous and an explosion of thoughts motivated my mind, my heart and soul. *Who is this person? What does she want? The way she looked at me on the way out, her face was shining. Was it love at first site? What does she want from me?*

She said, *I need to see you in person. It's very very important.*

I realized it must not have anything to do with Immigration, but although I had some ideas of what I hoped she wanted, I still had no idea. In any case, I dressed in my nicest casual clothes and my Drakkar Noir cologne. When we met at the rest stop on the Garden State Parkway, I was anxious and excited. When I walked in, I saw her sitting with a guy wearing a suit, which was immediately disappointing. I soon found out it was her husband, who was as nice as she was.

After shaking hands we sat down and she started complimenting me. *You have so much potential. I was very impressed by the way you handled yourself in court---the way you spoke to the judge, the way he talked to you. That's not an everyday thing.*

Then she asked if I knew anything about Amway, which I came to find out is a multi-level marketing company that sells different kinds of products. Even though she said, *You inspired me that day,* and told me that I could motivate people, I didn't really care. I knew I didn't want to sell anything because I didn't need a new career path. I was happy in the kitchen. I assumed every nice thing she had said to me up to that point was to encourage me to work with her.

I said, *I'm so confused right now about what to do, and I have to go back to Mexico. I'm not interested in selling.*

Then she asked if she could keep in touch with me. I didn't care because I was thinking I'd be gone within three months anyway.

174

Could you do me a favor? She handed me a cassette tape. *Listen to this tape and you'll get a better idea what I'm talking about.*

I thanked them both, said goodbye and left feeling like I had wasted time I would never get back. When I got in the car, I looked at the tape and something pushed me to pop it in the cassette player. As I began driving toward Asbury Park, I listened.

At the same time I thought about how disappointed I was and how much time I had spent wondering what she wanted with me. The other part of my brain was listening to the narrator's story about her success with Amway. Then someone else went on and on about the wonders of Amway and how shy he once was, and how working with the company helped him create a successful business and become more outgoing.

A couple of miles before I got home, the narrator switched again to a man named Gabriel, who said everyone used to tell him he was crazy for trying to make more of his life than having the regular job, kids and family life. But he had big dreams that had been squashed and he was ready to give up until he found Amway. He said, *Even my mother told me one day, Please stop chasing success and just be a regular person.*

But with Amway, he found the tools, the people and everything he needed to become the success he had always wanted to be. I remember looking out the window wondering if that's what I should do. Everyone was telling me it was time to go back to Mexico and relax. But Gabriel fueled me and made me believe I was hearing the tape for a reason and I shouldn't stop pursuing my dreams. That's what Amway did for me. I never sold a product, but it helped me recharge my battery. I decided to stop feeling sorry for myself and not give up. I listened to that tape a lot.

I got out of the car and said to myself, *Leo, one-two-three. Let's do it.*

Then I had a flash of brilliance. I thought of Filipe, my dear friend who had let me sleep on the flatbed of his pick-up truck while I recovered from my Freakardo/Freaknise disaster. I knew he was going through a very difficult time. He told me he had lost his construction job and even had to sell his truck to survive.

To make matters worse, his mother was very sick and he was the only one who could go to Mexico and take care of her. But his truck money didn't last and he couldn't even afford to eat, never mind travel. The thought of my friend with no job, no money, his sick mother and the way he stood and scratched his head trying to think of how to solve his problems, made me wonder what kind of miracle might happen to help him.

Then I thought of the American saying, "One hand washes the other." What if I bought him a plane ticket and gave him some money so he could go take care of his mother? I could do that. I had money for a plane ticket. But I was supposed to go to Mexico myself, although it seemed more important for him to go than it was for me to go. But what if Filipe pretended to be me? I could give him my birth certificate and have him get my plane ticket stamped and send it back to me so I would have proof that I went to Mexico without actually having to go. I loved the idea. It was the perfect crime. In fact, it was so perfect that it seemed like the kind of idea I might have seen in a movie like, *The Count of Monte Cristo*. But that would only work if my story was taken out of a book or a movie.

When I got back from Mexico, I needed to get my papers and a job. But I didn't want to work in the same area because I wanted to avoid bumping into negative souls like Freakardo and Freaknise. I thought of Edgar, a friend I had made at the Cypress Inn. It was great to have so many friends. I had bumped into him at the mall before my whole mess began. He

177

said he had gotten a job at a restaurant I'd never heard of. I couldn't remember the name of it and I'd never heard of the town it was in, but I knew it was near Freehold. As I was driving past Freehold into Manalapan, I saw a sign for Olde Silver Tavern and thought that might be it. Somehow by following my instincts I found it.

I went in and asked if Edgar worked there because I wasn't entirely sure I was at the right place. Not only did he work there, but Edgar came out and told Kenny, the chef, that I was a great worker. It was a very busy place, always in need of help, and I was hired on the spot.

The next day, I started my new job in the kitchen where I would work for the next two years. I was thrilled, but still fighting the feeling of defeat because of everything that had happened. My status issue was not completely solved and I felt funny telling Kenny, the boss, that I had applied for my papers, but didn't have them yet. Luckily, he didn't care.

Little by little, I found myself again. Bertha and I were back together and taking it slowly. She was trying to understand me and I appreciated it. She invited me to her new place one day, and it occurred to me that I should just be happy for what I had. Bertha wasn't like me, but I thanked God she wasn't like Freaknise. Bertha ended up going back to Mexico again, but at least this time we didn't end things on a sour note. We were broken up, but, we were still friends.

I made friends with another restaurant hostess I'll call Hope. She had long straight brown hair and would show up at work in what looked like pajama pants. Hope was an incredible person with a big heart. She was American, and although her mother was from Spain, she spoke almost no Spanish. She was two years older than I, and even though she was a single Mom, she was funny and happy.

We became very good friends, but in the beginning, our contact was limited to work. We would sit down together during lunchtime with our co-workers and laugh about everything and anything. It was easy to have fun with her. But I noticed every chance she got, Hope would sneak out to smoke. The more we got to know each other, the more I realized she liked beer a lot more than she should, and eventually I figured out she had a problem.

When I first came here I spoke no English and had no education. I had so much less than most people who live here. So whenever I met someone who didn't seem to be making the most out of life I'd think to myself: They have arms and legs. They're American. They speak English. They have everything! What's the problem? Why aren't they more successful?

Of course, I wasn't perfect either. I was young and learning new lessons all the time. One day I spent some time talking with Jimmy, one of my neighbors, who lived down the street. He was a positive person who also wanted to open a restaurant. I liked how I felt when I talked to other positive people and needed as many in my life as possible, and still do.

Jimmy offered me a drink, then another drink and many more. Before we knew it a lot of time had gone by. We lived on the same street, Fifth Avenue in Asbury Park, where I lived with Eduardo, who had said he would pick me up that day, but never showed up.

I got up to leave and felt the alcohol working on me. I told Jimmy I would be OK and got in the car to drive home, but I didn't go straight to my house. The car had a mind of its own and drove me to *La Bamba*, an old west bar, where I got even more drunk.

After closing the place at 2 a.m., I went looking for Freaknise in Eatontown. I sat in the parking lot and looked into her dark apartment. I went to the door and knocked on it hard. I called her name and there was no answer.

Thank God nobody came out because it would have been ugly. I wanted to say to her, *Why did you do this to me? I was there for you 100 percent. I don't understand how you could do something like that to someone like me!*

With a lot of the same anger I had when it first happened, I got back in the car. Even though I was disappointed that I didn't get a chance to give Freaknise a piece of my mind, I knew it was better that I didn't.

On my way home, while stopped at a light on Route 35, I distracted myself by fumbling with the radio dial looking for a song to cheer me up. Before I could settle on a station, I didn't notice the light had turned green, so the car behind me honked the horn. Then in the rearview mirror I saw flashing lights. I was getting pulled over.

Before I had time to worry about it, the cop came to the window of my 1989 Ford Cougar and asked for my credentials.

Officer, I'm drunk, I said.

Very nicely, he asked me to step out of the car. I said, *I don't usually drink, but I had a situation that made me want to drink.*

He didn't cuff me, but he did invite me to get into the back seat of his police car, which I knew I had no choice about. He explained that he had to take me back to the police station, and on the way, he asked me a lot of questions about my age, where I worked, where I was from and where I was going. I also told him about the Freakardo/Freaknise disaster and how heartbroken I was. I got the sense that he understood and felt at least a little bit bad for me because when we got to the station, he practically apologized for having to perform a breathalyzer test, and explained it was routine. He also said I would probably lose my license for about six months. I wasn't happy about it, but I understood.

After that, he asked, *Do you smoke?*

Sometimes, I said, and he motioned for us to go outside in a small area with a patio. When he handed me a cigarette, I felt like I was in a movie. According to the law, I would have to be detained for several hours before I could drive again. That's when he started telling me about his divorce. We obviously had a connection. He said never stop believing in love, but I should learn from my mistakes. He let me know that my situation was going to make me stronger and I shouldn't let it get me down. One of my lessons was not to drink and drive.

After he got those things off his chest, he said, *Look, you're going to lose your license, but there's no reason for me to keep you here.*

He called for another officer to take me home. Six months would seem like a long time not to have a driver's license, but I was glad I even had a license at all and that I would get it back.

Sometime after that, I went to a party, which I don't remember much about other than seeing Bertha there with another guy. She had come back again from Mexico like she always did, hoping we might get back together again.

I had gone to the party alone, but when I saw her I had no jealousy. I wanted her to be happy. I still felt defeated, now for new reasons, but I tried to block out the negativity. She came over to me and asked how I was doing. She introduced her friend to me and he seemed to know who I was. We kept talking and he eventually got bored and walked away.

When I asked why she wasn't going back to talk to him, she said, *I don't really care about that guy. I care about you.*

It made me feel good and bad at the same time. I didn't want to give her hope that we could be a couple again. I wanted to be done with that drama, but that's not what happened. She had moved into another apartment near my brother's house. She called me one day and wanted to talk. We were friends at that point. We had both gone through a lot of things and had grown in our own ways.

When I arrived at her apartment she had a couple of candles lit and a bottle of champagne. She was dressed nicely and seemed so sincere that I felt like I was seeing a brand new person with a different mentality. She had things to say in a way she hadn't before. I felt good being there. But when I think about it now, I wish I could remember more details. I wasn't 100-percent there. I couldn't be. My battery was still recharging from everything I had been through, therefore I wasn't conscious or present enough to have remembered if we ate anything or what we talked about. I do remember feeling safe and relieved when I was there with her, even though the past was still fogging my perspective. I knew it would be difficult to get rid of the feeling that we weren't meant to be. But maybe I had been wrong about us. I was confused. Still, I went back to Bertha's place again and again and enjoyed the comfort in spite of our past.

Not having my driver's license for six months was an experience that could have been worse. Getting to work every day was a challenge. I didn't want to move to Freehold to be closer to work. The best I could do was to take the bus from the Asbury Park Train Station to Freehold, and rollerblade three or four miles to Olde Silver Tavern. Sometimes I would stay at my friends' houses. Good people helped me out.

I never brought my problems to work, so no one really knew about my personal life. When I got to the tavern, as far as anyone else knew, I was Tony, a guy who cooked for people and made them laugh. I used my cousin's name because I wanted to be somebody else for a while without having to worry about anyone finding me. For the most part, it worked.

At the time I was staying with Bertha. I only had a few things, so even though I hadn't really moved in, it was as if I lived there. I walked in one day and she said, *I have great news.*

She very happily explained that she had taken a pregnancy test and it was positive. Her face was shining with excitement. I felt like I'd been shot in the head with information. It was the last thing I expected, but I was happy about it. My life was being decided for me or so it seemed, and I looked forward to being a father as a new chapter in my life. Things were suddenly beautiful between us. And then I told Bertha that my mother had gotten her visa and was coming to visit. I was very excited.

Bertha asked, *Where are you going to put her? Because there's no room for her in this apartment.*

I said, *She's just coming to visit.*

She said, *Then you'd better get her a hotel. And if you bring her here, I'll leave and you'll never get to see your son.*

I looked at her and said, *How can you say that? You're joking, right?*

And she said, *No, I'm not joking. I mean it.*

I felt like I had taken another punch and she was out of my heart again. I felt used and thought she must not care very much about me.

When I told my mother, she said, *Your first obligation is to your family. This is the woman you chose; you'd better be a man.*

It was true. Regardless of our differences, we were going to be parents. I wasn't sure what would happen next, but I was distracted with daily details in the meantime. I went from cook prep to working at the clam bar at the Tavern and it was a killer. The place was always packed with people. They sat behind the bar where Edgar made drinks and I was in the corner cooking. Kenny would say, *Tony, we need specials.*

He knew about my past experience and relied on me to introduce new dishes as specials. Edgar's ideas were also in demand because many of the other workers had limited experience.

One any given night, order tickets piled up so fast that I would have to put them on the counter and stuff them in my pockets. The whole time I cooked, there were people sitting at the bar talking to me and I felt like I was on display.

Once I became friends with all the workers, I thought about all the money the place had made and all the money I could be making as the owner. So I said to my other friends who worked there, *Why are we so stupid? Why don't we open our own business?*

They told me I was crazy. I knew that was at least partially true, but I also knew I was right! Still, it was depressing to think that I may never have my own business, so I refused to think that way. I was going to make it happen somehow.

Bertha had the chance to see me in action at work one night, functioning like an octopus. When we got out of there, she said, *I'm so proud of you. To see you back there, it's unbelievable. You're like a machine gun.*

I thanked her, but it bothered me. I'd been talking about how we should both strive to succeed and she was encouraging me to keep working for someone else, which wouldn't get us very far. She was cheering me on knowing how hard I had to work and how every night I'd come home hunched over in pain. I would blow my nose and the tissue would be black from the charcoal I had inhaled.

I said to Bertha, *I want something better. I don't want to be a machine gun. I want something different for us.*

To her it might just have been another one of my dreams that she didn't understand. My reaction was to lose myself in my work and focus on my daily routine. The next several months before my son Eric was born went by fast. Bertha's mother was coming from Mexico to be with her. When she told me, I didn't say anything.

When the time came, we went to the hospital and waited the whole day for Bertha to deliver. It was May 5, 1997. I was in shock after not sleeping for 24 hours, but I was also excited as well as concerned that the baby would be born in one piece. The doctor used forceps and I remember seeing my baby's head of black hair. His little body was being pushed out of Bertha's body and I saw his little face, then his shoulder and the rest of him slipping out. When the doctor asked me to cut the umbilical cord, I couldn't do it because I thought I might faint. We were so happy that Eric was born healthy. He cried as the nurses weighed him and cleaned him up. But then they started looking more closely at him because something was wrong. They said he had a condition, but I didn't understand exactly what they were saying, so I had no idea how serious it was or if it was serious at all. But I assumed it was because they said they had to keep him at the hospital and we couldn't take him home right away. Bertha didn't understand either. We just had to wait until they said he was OK. It turns out he had jaundice. Seven days later, we took him home to our apartment. Unlike most parents who start getting used to not sleeping right away, we had seven nights of sleep wishing our baby was home with us. Once we got him home, we didn't even want to sleep.

My mother was in Chicago with her brother and sister, and came to visit us three months after Eric was born. She lived with Eduardo and stayed here for two years to be with us and help out. I put my bad feelings aside the best I could even though the seed had been planted. I wasn't as happy with Bertha as I could have been. Even though it was a thrill to have a beautiful baby, I felt trapped.

When Eric was a year old, we had an argument and she invited me to pack up my clothes and leave. For the next two weeks, my Chevy Blazer was my suitcase and I stayed with different friends, but mostly with Eduardo and Mom. Eventually, Bertha invited me to come back and promised to change her attitude. I told her I would give our relationship another shot because I wanted to believe it was possible for the sake of our son. That night we went to a party and actually had fun dancing. But our happiness never lasted. No matter how hard Bertha and I tried---there was so much tension between us that never went away. One day when I was about to leave for work, she said, *If we're not going to be together I might as well go back to Mexico.*

I said, *Do what you have to do, but leave my son alone.*

She cried because she said she didn't think I believed her. After I went to work eight or nine hours later, I returned to an empty house. There was nothing left except a few of my things; no furniture or anything. It was even clean. There was a note written on a big piece of sketch paper in black marker on the clean empty floor that said: *I'm leaving. Don't worry about your son. He's going to be fine.*

She was taking him to Mexico and I didn't know when I would see him again.

I was not usually one to say no to a party, but when my sister invited me to celebrate Halloween with her I told her I was too sad to go. After talking a little bit I ended up going anyway. Sulking is not my thing. I felt better being out and talking to people, but after the party when I got home, I was sad again and fell asleep on the floor with nothing but a borrowed pillow and blanket from my sister's apartment.

I slept surprisingly well, but when I opened my eyes in the morning I wanted to cry because I missed Eric. He was my everything. Yet, I knew this was the beginning of a new chapter in my life. What I would do next was what I had always wanted to do, which was to go full force with my dreams. I wanted to work like I never had before and focus on the positive aspects of my life, rather than focusing on the pain. As soon as I did that, my luck changed.

One day at the Tavern, I made myself something for lunch and sat down for a break. Hope came and sat down next to me and asked how I was doing.

Things could be better. I explained what was on my mind.

She said, *I wish I could help you.*

Hope had her own troubles too. Money was tight because her child's father didn't pay child support. We started spending time together and talked about a lot of things. One day, she said, *I think we could make a good team. You are a nice guy. You're a very smart, hard-working person and that's something any woman would love. It's something I would love too.*

I didn't really know what she was saying because it came out of the blue. So I said, *Are you asking me to marry you? Because if you are, I hope you are sure that's what you want to do. It's a commitment.*

A few weeks later on my birthday, Sept. 5, 1997, without much preparation, we went to a courthouse in New York and stood before the judge in our nicest clothes. There we shared our first and only kiss. After that I applied for my working permit and realized Hope was right. We made a good team. But there were so many times that I wished things were different. It didn't take me long to figure out we were not compatible enough to live together, so I kept my own place and she kept hers.

Sometimes when it rains a lot and makes what looks like a river in the road, people try to drive through it with their cars. I have wondered what makes them think they can get through it. But at that time, I felt like one of those people in my car in the middle of a river and it was too late to turn around. I had to either correct it, or get out.

Out of nowhere, Robert Sweben told Andre to call me and ask if I would return to work at the Shadowbrook to replace someone in the banquet kitchen. I had been at the Olde Silver Tavern for two years, but I was happy to go back because a lot of the people at the Shadowbrook had become like family, including Andre, the secretaries, the cooks, wait staff and everyone else. The day I returned for an interview with Robert, it was as if nothing bad had happened. He agreed when I told him how much money I needed to make and that I had to have health benefits for my son. I also told him that I still had aspirations of having my own restaurant and planned to make it happen when the time was right. I am still grateful to him because of his support then and now. Since he sold the Shadowbrook in 2015, he spends most of his time in Florida, but when he comes home he likes to come to Chilangos to say hello.

Leo (far right) and his parents, Jose Cervantes, Abigail Soto Cervantes in the gated front courtyard of their home in Neza.

Chilangos

My co-worker Arturo thought of me when he found out about a small restaurant for sale in Long Branch.

He said, *Leo, your Mom is here, you have your brother and your sister, why don't you guys buy it and run it together?*

I remembered the place from when I took English lessons at Brookdale Community College's annex in Long Branch. Everyone used to go to *Café Mi Pueblito* on Third Avenue for coffee, soup and sandwiches.

Mom was still living with Eduardo in the apartment next to mine, so I went to tell her about it, and then I took her with me to check it out. When we met the owner, Maria, an older Chilean woman, I asked if she was selling it. Her eyes widened and she said, *Yes, why are you interested?*

She was asking $25,000. I said, *If you really wanted to sell it, how much would you want?* Then I asked if she would hold the note so we didn't have to go through the bank. She said, *The fact that you're here with your Mom is nice. I'll give it to you* *for $20,000 if you give me something down. Then you can make payments to me.*

I told Eduardo about the opportunity because I knew he had money to do it. He was excited! Since I didn't have money, I suggested he partner with Edgar from Colombia (my friend from Cypress Inn and Olde Silver Tavern), and I would work for them since Edgar also had money to invest. They both agreed until Eduardo changed his mind and offered to lend me the money so we could be partners. I was worried about Edgar feeling left out, but he understood. Because we were so close, and he was Eric's godfather, he only wanted what was best for me.

It didn't take much more than a month or two before we shook hands with Maria and took over the old *Café Mi Pueblito*. As we brainstormed for the name of our new business, we came up with *La Familia* or *Casa Cervantes*. When my sister suggested Chilangos, I thought it was perfect because back in time, people who came from other places to live in Mexico City were called Chilangos. Now, Chilango is a friendly nickname that means you're from Mexico City.

The responsibilities of running the place were divided among the five of us: Eduardo and Lorena, my sister Abigail, my Mom and me. The restaurant wasn't perfect. It needed to be cleaned up in every way, even the clientele. They would bring in cases of beer when there was a game on TV. When we didn't allow it anymore, they had to go someplace else. There was no liquor license either, just food. Our new clientele, which was entirely Latino and mostly Mexican, found us quickly when we opened for lunch and dinner. We made enchiladas, *pozole*, seafood soups, tacos, tamales, quesadillas and gorditas.

After dropping my Mom off at the restaurant in the morning, I would go get supplies for the day and handle the paperwork, prep the food and take care of the social aspect of the business, while everyone else did their jobs.

Then I'd go work at the Shadowbrook, cook for the employees and, if I didn't have a party, I could go back to Chilangos and do whatever needed to be done there. It made me so happy. I was working like a crazy person, but it seemed worth it. The whole experience brought me back to our days at ANEAL, my family's convenience stores in Neza. One of the reasons I was so excited about Chilangos was because it was a way for us to spend time together as a family and do something good. On a typical day we made between $200 and $350. When we made $500, we were very happy. But I remember one Saturday we went crazy because we made $1,000.

I learned some lessons about the legal aspects of the business the hard way because I didn't know any better. After announcing our grand opening in the Asbury Park Press, a town official came and wanted to see our licenses.

Very innocently, I asked, *Was I supposed to have licenses?*

I really didn't know, but I quickly found out. I had this wall in front of me and I had to get on the other side. The cooking part of Chilangos I could manage, but the legal side of the business and the paperwork was something I had never done before. It was tough and I went through a lot in the two years we owned Chilangos in Long Branch, which was my school for business. Cypress and Shadowbrook were my schools for cooking. It made me think of swimming lessons and how the instructor holds you while you learn to kick and stroke your arms. Running Chilangos was like being thrown in the ocean. The only difference was that I had thrown myself in the water without knowing how to swim.

I remember one day I went to borough hall in Long Branch and someone, although I don't remember who he was, started rattling off a list of things I needed to do, like file permits and hire an accountant and pay taxes, and the list seemed endless.

I didn't know anything! It's easier now because I have help with every aspect of the business to make it run smoothly. It's a long list of resources that took a long time to build.

The first accountant we hired created a disastrous mess that cost about $30,000 in penalties to fix, even though he came recommended by another business owner, who also became a victim of the accountant's ignorance. Still, it wasn't the end of the world, just an expensive lesson. The moral of that story is sometimes you don't know what you're getting into and bad things can happen even if you think you're being smart. The even bigger lesson is to avoid having your dreams squashed by things like that. People who focus on the difficulties of owning a business should realize it doesn't make it any more dangerous than working for someone else whose business goes under or has trouble and affects you as an employee. If you want to do your own thing, you have to be mentally prepared for the ups and downs. The good news is there are many more ups than downs in my opinion.

After three months at Chilangos, Eduardo wasn't happy because he believed he was working too hard and making too little to justify it. Just as I had kept my job at the Shadowbrook, he kept his construction job to support his wife Lorena and daughter, Erika, who was born about two weeks after Eric was born. After going back and forth about it, we decided that I would keep the business and pay him back his initial investment. I knew it was the best thing for the family.

I was very happy the day I received a working permit in the mail from Homeland Security. The front apartment in the house my brother lived in happened to be vacant, so I moved in. The owners of the house had asked me before if I wanted to buy the house, but whether I wanted to or not didn't matter. I couldn't do it in the past because I had no credit, no green card and no way to make it happen. But suddenly, I had a working permit and the prospect for residency since I was married to Hope.

We waited for a year before being interviewed by Immigration for the application for my residency. We were the last ones to be seen. The interviewer yelled, *Cervantes!*

We went into his office and he pulled a huge file from his desk. Hope, my lawyer and I approached him and asked how he was, but the mostly bald-headed man didn't answer. His tie looked like a colorful rollercoaster draped over the big hill of his belly covered in a white dress shirt. *These are the cases I hate the most,* he said.

I had applied for political asylum, a deportation procedure, and a complicated history. I looked at the lawyer and then at Hope, who both had what I call "the diarrhea face," which means something bad is coming, you have to deal with it and there's no escaping it. I knew he wanted to take me out, but I had to be calm, so I counted *one-two-three* and took a deep breath to prepare for whatever was coming.

OK, Mr. Cervantes. You came in 1989 with a visitor's visa, right? His tone was sarcastic. *Then, you applied for political asylum. Is that right? Then your status was changed from political asylum to being sponsored by your employer.*

Yes, sir.

Then you postponed your court hearing, then you postponed it again, and you came to your last hearing, and you signed a paper stating that you would go back to Mexico voluntarily. Is that right, Mr. Cervantes?

He showed me the paper. *Is that your signature?*

Yes, sir.

OK, Mr. Cervantes. Then you came back and now your new application is based on marriage.

As he opened the file, Hope asked, *What would you like to know about our marriage?*

He looked at Hope and said, *Before we talk about your marriage, I have one simple question for you, Mr. Cervantes.*

His bald-headed spotlight was now on me. He said, *If you can prove to me that you went back to Mexico, we can move forward with your new application. If you're not able to prove to me that you left the country, unfortunately, your marriage application means nothing.*

My lawyer was there as a shield, but he didn't really know what to expect. He and Hope both sat there with the same diarrhea faces staring at me as I reached down to my briefcase on the floor and said, *I don't know why and I don't know how, but I've been saving this for a long time.*

I handed the bald man my stamped airplane ticket and his eyes popped wide open. I was like a magician pulling a green card out of my sleeve.

Mr. Cervantes, you know if this paper is fake I could throw you in jail before I deport you to Mexico!

Yes, sir, I understand that.

He looked at it again and then went to his computer, which I knew was just for show because he didn't know what to do. He said, *I was supposed to either give you a green card or send you back to Mexico, but I'm not going to make this easy on you. I'm only going to give you a temporary stamp on your passport until your lawyer gets me a letter from the airline verifying that the ticket is real.*

On the way out, my lawyer, who was quite useless in the situation, wanted us to pose with the small Statue of Liberty in the waiting room of the Immigration office. So I posed and smiled as I was thinking that I had just won a small battle, but not the entire war.

You did a great job, he said. But really, I had done it all.

About two months later my green card arrived in the mail. My first concern was making plans to go see Eric. Things were improving in some ways and getting worse in others. I was having bad dreams because I had so much anger that Bertha had taken Eric away. People who cared about me said I should call the FBI because she took my son without my permission. That's kidnapping. But I didn't. Instead, I made arrangements with Bertha to go to Mexico to see him.

I went to Bertha's house and knocked on the door. When she opened it, her face lit up as if she wanted to hug me. But I spotted Eric at the end of the hallway behind her.

I said, *Hi, Eric!* He looked at me and looked down. That really hurt. Then she called to him and said, *Say hello to your Daddy.*

We had been apart for several months; he was just two. I wanted to take him to different places in Mexico, like *El Rancho* to visit family in Guanajuato. She smirked when I tried to hold him and he reached out to her. She seemed to enjoy every second of it. When took him by the hand and he started crying for his Mommy, I knew I had to take her with us so he would be happy.

When Eric was three, Bertha came back to the U.S. because she had a visa and found a place to live a couple of blocks from me. I was so happy to have Eric back. I could see him going through what I went through when I was kid, having my father in and out of my daily life. But the difference was that Eric and I were very much attached. We were always playing together. I would dress him up like a football player or put a bandana on his head. I even put a red dress on him and a headband with a flower just for fun. To this day, he loves the Beatles because I used to listen to them a lot. He loved to dance to the music. We

Leo and Eric at the Pyramids in Teotihuacan, Mexico City.

had a lot of good times together and he grew up knowing how to have fun.

When my Mom was in the U.S., she would take care of Eric when he was with me and I was working. It was hard for me to leave the house sometimes because he didn't want me to go. He would hold my arm and cry when he knew I had to leave and I'd have to distract him somehow, and then sneak out. I hated doing that, but otherwise I would never have been able to go anywhere without him. But once again, Bertha threatened to go back to Mexico for good and eventually, although not until Eric was much older, she left and I had no choice but to let them go.

Hope and I admitted that we weren't really compatible, though we had tried, and agreed to give each other freedom. As they say, one door closes and another one opens.

In 2001, some co-workers from the Shadowbrook invited me on a trip to Colombia. I had been introduced to a new server at the Shadowbrook---a Colombian girl named Jenny Correa. She didn't seem thrilled to meet me until she heard I was going to her home country. She asked if I would pick up a piece of luggage from her mother's house in Colombia and bring it back to her. I agreed and that's how we became friends. She was pretty and kind of quiet and shy, but very nice. I found out how much she liked to dance when I was invited to a welcoming party thrown for her in Long Branch.

Another time we went dancing at a party to benefit someone who had been in an accident, and something happened that surprised Jenny. Two thieves wearing ski masks came to steal the money that was raised. One of them had a gun and scared everyone so much that some guests ran out. I took Jenny and we slid under a table. One of the other guests picked up a chair and swung it at one of the thieves. Then everybody started running after them. Luckily, the lady in charge threw the box of money under a table and the thieves ran out before getting it. It was a terrible introduction to the U.S. Jenny didn't think things like that happened here.

Even though Jenny had earned a college degree in finance in Colombia, she came to the U.S. hoping it would be easier to find a job than it was in her home country. We had something in common. She knew what it was like to live in the jungle. She was born in Medellin, Colombia and lived there until her father lost his job driving a truck for a frozen food company. Jenny was about 8 at the time and after being evicted from the house they rented, the family moved in with Jenny's grandfather in

Campo Baldes, where it was dangerous to be outside after dark unless you wanted to risk being shot at for no good reason.

Jenny told me, *We could hear gunshots at any time of the day and it was normal. We could see gangsters and drugs right out in the open.*

It sounded a lot like Neza. Her mother was traumatized because before they moved in with her grandfather, they lived in a quiet town. Jenny says, *She wasn't used to it. She would listen to the shots and tell us to get down on the floor or go hide.*

Jenny was taking a shower once and saw someone's face looking in the bathroom window. It was a scary place to be at the time. When she was about 15, she was almost kidnapped on her way home from school. She had to walk about eight blocks to the public bus stop and saw a car pull into the entrance of a parking garage. The driver got out and yelled to her, *Get in!* She ran like crazy for about half a block until she came to a hospital where she hid near the security guard. After 20 minutes or so, she blended in with other people and walked back out into the street.

When she was in college the danger was so distracting it was hard for her to concentrate on studying, so her father put a light in her three-by-three bedroom closet, where she would sit cross-legged underneath the hanging clothes and next to her shoes, with her books and notebooks in her lap.

Even though the situation improved when Pablo Escobar died in 1993, she still wanted to leave Colombia because she had hopes of working and sending money back to her parents to help their family live a better life, which is exactly what she did. Eventually, they were able to move to a better neighborhood.

When we met I thought she must be lonely because even though she was living with friends in Long Branch, she was here without her family. She had only been here a month, but I could tell something was bothering her. I thought she might be homesick. The Superman part of my personality wanted to be her friend, make her laugh or do whatever I could to make her happy.

The more time I spent with Jenny, the more I liked her, and the more comfortable we became together. She was very focused on me and I liked that, but now I realize I had her attention mainly because she had no one else to give it to.

She told me about a situation she was having with the family she lived with. They had only been her neighbors in Colombia, but since they were altogether in the U.S., they wanted to take care of her. But Jenny, who was 24 at the time, wanted to be more private and left to do her own thing. I understood. She told me she wanted to move out of their house, but didn't think she could afford to live alone. I wasn't looking for a girlfriend because I didn't want to get distracted from my work or my goals, but I didn't see anything wrong with inviting her to move in with me in the house in Asbury Park. She would be my roommate just like I'd had other roommates in the past. But it didn't turn out that way. When we moved in together we were a couple and I was very happy.

On weekends, Jenny worked at the Shadowbrook and in the afternoon she would help me at Chilangos. She believed in my dream and saw it as an opportunity. That was also very attractive to me at the time. She had a job as a housekeeper in a private house. I was so determined to become successful in my business that I had passion pouring out of my ears. Just the fact that I was able to open a business made me automatically successful. It didn't matter what might happen after that. But I wanted to build it and feel even happier. I was dedicated to Chilangos and knew if I stayed on that path I would get somewhere.

While I was at work at the Shadowbrook one day, Jenny met Bruce Springsteen's personal chef, Jacob, who came to Chilangos to eat. He really liked the food so he came back again, but I didn't know who he was. When he introduced himself as Bruce's personal chef, I said, *Yeah, and my uncle is George Bush.* He said, *No really. It's true.*

Jenny and Leo at Chilangos in 2002
when they first opened. Notice the sign
in the background that says, "God Bless
America."

We became friends, but lost touch and I didn't think anything of it, although I liked him a lot.

After about one year in business, Jenny and I received a promotional postcard from a realtor about Madeline's, an Italian restaurant for sale in Highlands. I had only been to Highlands to buy seafood from the Lusty Lobster for certain dishes we made at the restaurant. From what I knew, there was nothing else to do in the town of Highlands. But I didn't let that discourage me, and my open-mindedness paid off.

When I walked in to Madeline's Italian Restaurant, it was love at first site. I knew it would be the new Chilangos. The bars and the floors were shiny black granite. The place was clean, which took my attention away from the size and the fact that it was very dark inside. I had a vision of orange, green and yellow---colors to brighten the place and represent Mexico.

The second time we went to Madeline's we sat down to eat. The owners were real-deal Italians and the pasta was good. We went to visit a total of three times to check it out and talk to the owner. When Madeline decided she liked us and wanted us to have it, I told her my situation, and she suggested I would have a good chance of getting an SBA loan if I applied for one. She even lowered the price to make it more possible for us. I was excited and started saving money for a down payment while I waited to find out if I could get a loan.

In the meantime, between the two of us, Jenny and I had five jobs. We were about halfway through the process of getting accepted for the loan when the World Trade Center in New York City was attacked on September 11, 2001, and everything stopped. From that point, it took another nine months to get the money from the bank. When someone else approached Madeline about buying her place, she let me know it and started putting some pressure on me. Still, because she wanted me to have it, she told the interested person that she was holding it for someone else.

While I was at the Shadowbrook one day, my Mom told me about a man named Gary who showed up at Chilangos in Long Branch to eat. My Mom fed him a plate of ribs with green tomatillo sauce and cactus, and from that day forward he became a steady representation of my one percent of American clientele. He also happened to be the person who wanted to buy Madeline's. When Madeline finally told him I was the prospective buyer, he bowed out because he loved Chilangos and wanted to see me in a bigger place.

By 2002, Jenny and I had known each other for a year when I got the loan and bought the new Chilangos. We kept the Long Branch restaurant going for about six months until I offered to sell it to Lina, one of my workers, who loved the idea of being a business owner, but had no money. Because I had been given opportunities and wanted to give her the opportunity, I held the note until she was able to pay me back. She changed the name to *Tres Fronteras*.

I was happy to be able to focus on the new Chilangos. The first thing we did was paint, which took two months because it was January. The whole thing was tough because the minute we bought the place, we started shelling out money to fix it up. We didn't make much from Chilangos in Long Branch before Lina completely took over and we had to live on the $700 a week or so I was making at the Shadowbrook, plus whatever Jenny made. All in all, it was difficult, but we were able to do it because we were lucky enough to have so many family members and friends to lend us money. I am grateful to all of them.

Jenny and I worked really hard to get the business going. We all did a little bit of everything. Whenever there was a need, Jenny could be a bartender or server. She also made cakes and made the menus. We were lucky to have good people working with us from day one. My friends from Asbury Park---Enrique and his wife, Mireya, from Mexico---came to cook for us. Then Javier and Thomas were in the kitchen until they went back to Mexico. Monica Loyola from Acapulco was here for three or four years. She was a lovely saint-like person to me, so I named Enchiladas Santa Monica for her, which are chicken enchiladas with *pasilla* sauce.

If you've been to Chilangos recently, you might know about or have met Geovanny Calderon from Costa Rica, who worked at the restaurant called Havana down the street and used to come here to eat until he eventually started cooking for me five years ago. Tatiana Baros from Colombia and Diana Fragoso from Mexico are two of my servers, who both worked at The Quay in Sea Bright before it closed, and have now been here longer than anyone else. Then there's Juan Trejo, the bartender from Mexico, who has been with me since we opened. I will also never forget Mayra Barreto, another bartender who worked with me on and off for nine years and is still one of my best friends. Margarita and Ricardo, mother and son also from Mexico, are in the kitchen now and my Mom also cooks when she visits. In fact, you can tell when she's here by my weight gain.

Geovanny and Mayra, co-workers at Chilangos.

I am passionate about feeding and entertaining people, so it makes me happy to be able to say thank you to all the people who have been with me from the beginning.

During my next visit to Mexico, I was also happy to find out Jenny had thrown up one morning. She thought she might be pregnant since she's not one of those people who throws up for no reason. I was in Mexico because Alejandro had called to say our father had come home again after being away for the better part of 10 years. During those 10 years, we probably heard from him or saw him about 10 times. This time he would be home for a while, rather than just a quick hello and goodbye. He needed to rest and heal after getting into a fight with a group of people who made him think were his friends. He had been stabbed, but we didn't know and would never know the whole story. We didn't press him for the details. All we could do was support him while he got better.

When Jenny called me I wasn't really thinking about the reality that she might be pregnant. I was distracted by the fact that it had been a long time since I'd seen my Dad. When we saw each other, we hugged and I was happy to see him. When I asked why he'd stayed away for so long, he said, *You know I have problems with your Mom.*

217

I said, *I have problems with Eric's mother, but I'm here in Mexico to see my son.*

Still, I was happy to have the somewhat unbelievable treat of seeing most of my family, including my Dad, but excluding Abigail and Eduardo, who were in the U.S. My Dad was 63 by then. He was always thin, but now he was thinner than ever. His teeth were worn down and his hair was mostly gone. The little hair he had left was gray to match his eyebrows. I still think of him wearing the polo shirt with brown and tan squares. I knew he was very happy to be home too, although he was never outwardly happy like I am. He had so much guilt that he couldn't relax. He was always holding back. I could feel it. But I knew he was doing better than he had in a while because he was in AA dealing with his alcohol problems, and he realized the people he thought were his friends were actually very sick. He wanted to help them. He asked how Abigail and Eduardo were doing in the U.S. They were fine. Eduardo was working construction. *Chica*, as we called my sister, was living in an apartment in the same house I lived in Asbury Park.

Jenny, I found out, was definitely pregnant. I was very excited about having a baby with her because I thought it was my chance to have the family I'd always wanted. To me, life itself is an opportunity to experience something new every day. I saw her pregnancy as a natural next step in our relationship.

While in Mexico, it was nice to have my Mom's cooking to look forward to each day. She made my favorite---pig's feet and enchiladas. Alejandro was there, my nieces and nephews, my sister Noemi and my father. It was such a good feeling that something I had always wished I could have was now right in front of me. But even though I was grateful for that, the past was still there to haunt me.

While my Dad and I were talking one afternoon, he was suddenly startled by the time. It was almost 2'oclock---time to pick up my nephew--Alejandro's oldest son, Omar---from school. I offered to join him on the walk through Neza about six blocks from the house. When we found Omar, that's when it hit me.

I said, *How nice this is?* He asked what I meant. *You probably wouldn't know,* I said.

Again, he asked what I was talking about. As we walked back home, I couldn't help the jealousy and even anger that came up when I said, *It must be nice for Omar to have you to pick him up from school and walk home with him.*

What's the big deal?

I said, *You never did that for me.* Tears popped out of my father's eyes and I immediately felt bad. Then he tried to blame it on the problems he had with my Mom again.

I said, *What did that have to do with me?*

He said, *I know, please forgive me.*

I said, *I don't have anything to forgive you for. But did I do anything to you to make you not want to see me?*

There was nothing he could say. I didn't want Omar to hear, so I dropped it.

The next day, I said to Dad, *Let's forget about yesterday and talk about positive things. There's something I want to do. It's something I've wanted for a long time.*

He said, *Anything you want.*

I'm going to buy a piece of property and I'd like you to be the general contractor and build a house on it for all of us. Can you do that?

He agreed and we shook hands. In the morning I left Mexico feeling reborn somehow because I could see my family together in my mind. Just imagining it made me feel so good when I returned to the U.S. and gave me energy when I came back to work at Chilangos.

The next beautiful occasion was Gabriela's birth on July 16, 2003. I was so happy to have a healthy little girl. She is now 12 and surprises me every day with her intelligence and sense of humor.

So many things happened in 2003. After seven years, Hope and I agreed to get divorced with absolutely no hard feelings. Even though I wasn't anxious to be rid of her, I was happy to be free. Because she was always nice to me and understanding, she proved to me that there are still good people in the world. I will always be grateful that she was part of my life.

I'm constantly meeting interesting people at Chilangos. So many good conversations happen over meals because food is the connection. Especially in my case---without food and my recipes and my background---I wouldn't know half the people I know now.

Certain dishes have greater connecting power than others, which is what I discovered when I made shrimp stuffed with cream cheese, breaded with coconut and sesame seeds. I rolled tortillas and stuffed them with chicken breast and Oaxaca cheese, and breaded them with the same sesame and shredded coconut combination, topped with tomato sauce and corn. By combining those flavors, calling it sesame and coconut *flautas*, I have made a lot of friends.

Someone came in one day and said, *I should bring my good friend here who is also from Mexico City and loves tequila.* He said, *He happens to be Bruce Springsteen's personal chef.*

Jacob? I said, *I know Jacob.*

When we saw each other again he suggested "the Boss" might like to have the annual Christmas party for his employees at Chilangos. I respect people for what they do and what they represent, but to me an artist is just a person like me, so I didn't get nervous when Bruce and Patti came to Chilangos for the party. I don't respect them for what they have, but rather for what they are. Bruce is such a down-to-earth guy, and I've learned that he's also a man who cares about people and takes care of his family.

Leo and Bruce at Chilangos in Highlands.

During the party, he thanked me very sincerely. I found out how much respect he has for immigrants, when he cared enough to ask me how I made my way here. I told him that I came from Mexico City where I grew up very poor, where my friends became gangsters, and that I came here to make a better life for myself, and started working at a place called the Cypress Inn.

I asked him, *Do you remember that place?*

He said, *Yes, how did you know?*

Because one day there was a lot of excitement, so I asked my friend Manny, Que pasa? What's going on?

He said, *El jefe esta en la casa. That's why everyone is excited.*

The boss is in the house? The boss is always in the house. What's the big deal?

He said, *No! There's a famous singer named Bruce Springsteen and he's here tonight. That's why everyone's happy.*

About an hour later, everyone gathered at the window and Manny called me over. He said, *You see that guy getting inside that van? That's Bruce Springsteen.*

I said, *Oh, OK. Great. Let me go back and wash my dishes.*

Bruce was laughing. *You didn't know who I was?*

I said, *No!*

I love your story, he said. *See? Isn't life funny? Now we're doing shots of tequila.*

Then he pointed to my Mom and asked who she was. I introduced them and he hugged and kissed her and told everyone to thank her for cooking for them. It was funny because she had no idea what he was saying or that he is super-famous. She just thought he was one of my friends. Actually, by the end of the night, he was my new friend.

After that I cooked for the Springsteen family a few times for some of their house parties, and eventually I started filling in for Jacob when he took time off. All I can tell you is the Springsteen family are beautiful, wonderful people, who bring a lot of people a lot of happiness. Being in their company was always interesting and fun.

There was no time that it was clearer to me than in 2004, the importance of positive thinking and living. My Mom had come to visit in October and left six months later. When she got back to Mexico, my father had stopped in to see her on his way to Guanajuato, the town of his birth. His sister was sick and needed someone to take care of her, according to one of his relatives. My mother's sister came from Chicago and met her in New Jersey before they went back to Mexico together. From there, they had planned on taking a trip to Michoacán to a friend's wedding. Before they left, they saw my father. While they were saying goodbye, he told my aunt, *Please take care of her.*

She said, *Yes, I always do.*

My Mom asked, *Why are you so worried about me all of a sudden? It's been 25 years that you haven't cared about me.*

He said, *Because I may never see you again.*

Then he asked my aunt for a hug. She said, *When we come back from our trip, we'll get together.*

They left on April 14. On May 4, I had been getting ready for Cinco de Mayo and it was 1 a.m. by the time I was cleaning up and setting the tables for the next day. The Chilangos business phone rang. I had a funny feeling hearing it ring because there's usually no good news at 1 a.m.

A voice said, *Leo?*

Alejandro? How's Mom? Is she OK?

She's fine. But, Dad....

I said, *What happened?*

He died. He was in a car accident.

I could tell by his voice there was something more. I said, *Tell me the truth.*

That is the truth, he said.

I wouldn't believe it.

Finally, he gave in. *I'm going to tell you. You remember when he went to take care of his sister?*

He reminded me that Dad had been friends with a gang of bad guys who were angry with him. When Dad decided to clean himself up and stop drinking, he tried to talk them into doing the same. But they didn't appreciate his judgment and told him if they ever saw him in Guanajuato again, he would be sorry.

Alejandro said, *He was out buying medicine for his sister when he bumped into them, and as promised, they killed him.*

When he said that, I flashed back on our plans to build the house and our promise, like a movie in my head. I started crying. I didn't even know why I was crying so much. My father was almost never there.

I hung up and called home. Jenny answered, but she was short with me. So I didn't tell her about my Dad. When I got home she could see I was crying and I explained why.

The next day when I went to Chilangos, I stayed in the kitchen all day. It wasn't until the end of the night that I finally came out, grabbed a bottle of tequila and went table by table doing shots with everybody.

I talked to Mom about it. She was called to identify Dad's body at the morgue. It was my father's niece who had called my brother with the news. They believed Dad was run over by a car. But when Mom and Alejandro got to the morgue, they were told his body had been destroyed and may be difficult for them to see.

The mortician said, *The way he died wasn't easy. There is no way a car hit him. The damage to the body had to have been caused by rocks or some other hard objects. Even his face needed reconstructing. He was most definitely murdered.*

So they opted not to see his body to avoid remembering him that way. Circumstances had been harsh enough. Mom was sad about it, but she was more worried about me and how I was feeling. She said, *I know it's been hard for you.*

It was true, but there was nothing we could do but move on. It took me three days to process what had happened. I accepted my Dad's choices and the way he lived his life. I know that if you don't learn from your mistakes, you have a big problem. I knew I could not live with such sadness in my head. My father was born in 1940 and lived until 2004. He made wrong choices and that's how he ended up: wrong. I had to be honest about it. That's why I felt so strongly about being positive and doing positive things.

My pain went away May 10, 2005 when Emiliano, my third child, was born. He is 10 now and reminds me of myself as a kid because I liked food so much. He eats like a monster. He was so cute when he was little. Until he went to kindergarten, he refused to speak Spanish. I would say, *Hable español.* But he would shake his head no. So one day I figured out how to fix his problem. I invited my Mom, who spoke no English (and still doesn't), to come spend time with us. It only took about a month before he started speaking Spanish.

The same year, Jenny and I got married at our house by my friend Dennis Leppard, a reverend---just the two of us and the kids. It represented a new beginning in our relationship.

Because our kids were already born I didn't see marriage as a necessary thing like many people do. But Jenny did, so it was a way to give her security and make one of her dreams come true.

In 2006, I filled out my paperwork to become a citizen, which I accomplished two years later. The following year, Bertha wanted to take Eric back to Mexico. He was 10 and I didn't really want him to go because I believed he could have a better life here. But I agreed to let her take him on one condition: I would take him to Mexico to see if he wanted to stay once he got there. I wanted to make sure it felt right. All I wanted was for him was to grow up well. Because he had Bertha's family there, cousins and aunts and uncles, he was excited about it and wanted to get to know them, which I thought was as important as understanding his culture and mastering Spanish. I wasn't looking forward to saying goodbye to him, but I was very pleased that he would have new experiences and the chance to embrace my culture, which would soon be his too.

In 2008, I felt like I needed to make something happen--- something new. When I found out about a club for sale in Paterson, my new business partner and I went to talk to the owners and strike a deal. When it came time for my partner to come up with his money, he couldn't do it. But once again, I got lucky. I told the owners what happened and since they wanted me to have the business, they offered to hold the note.

My idea was to change what was already a nightclub called Laura's into something more special. Before I bought it, only Colombian people went there, but I wanted to make it more diverse so everyone felt welcome. One night a guy walked up to the bar where I was sitting to ask if he could request a song for the DJ to play. He wrote something down on a cocktail napkin and gave it to me to give to DJ Pedro. After that, I went downstairs and Pedro came down to ask when he could announce the new name of the club. I told him I didn't know what it should be, but that I was considering Club 33.

Pedro said that was kind of funny because the guy with the napkin requested a song from an old band called 33. I had never heard of them, but I told him the number 33 had been chasing me. Pedro's friend, Ricardo, who happened to be a numerologist, told me the significance of the number three. Every number has some significance, of course, but three has to do with creativity, optimism and growth, relates to the Trinity, the energy of the "creator" and enthusiasm for living life to the fullest.

When I finally decided to change the name of the club about six months later, it was partly because a lot of the customers were police officers. I thought it would be cool for the club to be called Precinct 33. I even bought a 2006 black and white police car, which matched the black and white interior of the nightclub where the bar was actually behind bars, and the dancers, bouncers and bartenders wore police uniforms. I used the police car for advertising.

I noticed the number 33 everywhere for about two years---from the microwave to the TV to the clock in the car. The craziest one was the day Barrack Obama won the Presidential election. I was going to Bruce Springsteen's house to cover for Jacob. We had a babysitter at the time. She said, *Leo, you're going to Bruce's house? Would you mind driving me to the Red Bank train station?*

We jumped in the car and as we were driving there, she suggested I play 33 in the lottery. But I didn't really believe in that. She was determined to make me see what was happening.

She asked, *How many kids do you have?*

I said, three.

How old is Emiliano?

He's three.

She asked when I was born. *September 6, 1969.*

She said, *September is the ninth month. Three times three is nine. Three plus three is six and 1969 is all broken down to threes.*

How old is Jenny?

She was 33.

She said, *See! Maybe there's something to it.*

I said, *Holy shit! Let me call Jenny.*

I had a flip phone. When I opened it up the time was 3:33.

When my psychic friend, *El Niño Prodigio,* came to the nightclub and we talked about the number chasing me, he said, *Don't be afraid of it. It's God and angel Gabriel. You're a very lucky guy. You might hit the lottery one day.*

Two or three months later, I went to the club with a friend of mine named Jason. On the way back, we stopped at Quick Check on Route 36. We went in the store to buy coffee or soup or something. The jackpot was $280 million. Jason suggested I play.

Why? I asked.

Because you're very lucky.

I said, *I'll only buy a ticket if it gets to $333 million.*

He looked over and said, *Holy shit, Leo. Look above your head!*

I turned around and there was a sign that said, "Buy three Coca Colas for $3.33."

Two or three days later, *El Niño Prodigio* called me from Miami, telling me to buy a ticket because the jackpot was up to $333 million. I was shaking when I went to the store to buy 33 tickets. I didn't win the jackpot, but I did hit three numbers on one ticket and won $88.

I loved having the club because of three things: It was full of happy people, I enjoyed the loud music, and being able to see and talk to everyone. Unfortunately, the economy slowed the business down, so I took an opportunity to get out when the old owners wanted it back. So many things were closing, even big chain stores like Home Depot, so I had to get rid of it. I'll bet you can guess how many years I had the business. Three!

Now I realize that one of the reasons I was meant to have that business was to meet two very important people. I've always felt very lucky, but I really believe you make your own luck. In 2010, I was at Precinct 33 when a young man approached me.

Janny Torres introduced himself as a fan of Chilangos. He and his brother Marco Torres, also from Mexico City, were singers in need of a manager. They did well and had a lot of recognition with their last manager, but any money they made, he took and then took off. They had been shopping for a new manager to represent them and they believed I was the man for the job.

At the time, they sang a style of music called Bachata-Dominican and had appeared on the Don Francisco show called *Sabado Gigante*. They showed me the video and I realized I had seen it already because I remembered that I didn't like it. What I did like was a bit of personal information they shared with Don Francisco: Their mother knew it was their dream to be on that show, but she died before she was able to see it happen.

I told them that while I was flattered that they wanted me, I didn't know anything about the music business and I didn't believe my appreciation of music was enough. It was Jenny who said, *Leo you should do it*. It wasn't that I didn't believe I could do it, but I didn't want to mislead these two brothers who had a dream and needed guidance about how to make it come true.

I knew they were talented, but from what I had seen on TV, they needed new material. When I accepted the challenge of becoming their manager, the first thing we did was to record a new CD and make a music video. The very minute I knew I would be traveling with them to Miami, California, Mexico, Chicago and Colombia, I knew I was in the right business. Learning a new industry by getting to know the people involved was fun for me and I took to it very quickly.

Janny and Marco's publicist was Adolfo Fernandez, and we went to meet him in Miami to discuss our new plans. After being introduced, we sat down and Adolfo's dog, a pug named Poty (Poh-tee), walked into the office and fell asleep on my legs.

Adolfo said, *You must be a very special person because I've had thousands of people here and he usually hides from everyone.*

His assistant, Ricardo, was the only other person the dog was comfortable enough to fall asleep on. So I said, *We must be connected.*

I was half kidding, but I didn't know why else the dog would climb up my leg and fall asleep on me. We talked about their style of music, which was pure Bachata, and came up with the idea to combine Bachata with Mariachi and call it Bachata-Mex, a completely new style that started a new trend. Other bands followed our lead and began infusing the two sounds. When I said we would shoot a new video, Adolfo offered to put some

Marco Torres, Leo and Janny Torres.

money toward it because he was excited about Janny and Marco's new direction.

Since then, they have enjoyed more recognition with four new music videos you can see on YouTube. They've also been on CNN Español and every Latino TV show in the U.S., and most recently City TV in Colombia.

The same year, JannyMarco (as they are known) sang at the formal wedding Jenny and I decided to have at the Shadowbrook to celebrate our lives together with 200 of our closest friends and family members. It was beautiful to see Jenny so happy. That was the most important thing, to see her face glowing. The second most important thing was being with all my friends and family and everyone who meant something to me. It was a Jenny moment, but it was also a Leo moment.

I got a taste of what it was like to have two businesses at once in 2012, when the owner of the local ferry company I'll call Freakstreak asked me to do a version of Chilangos on the beach in Highlands, where commuters get on and off the ferry. I loved the idea of being on the beach in the summer and having an outdoor venue, although it was hard to be in two places at once.

Luckily, I had the help and enthusiasm of Gerilyn Fiore. Her sister, Michelle, was a friend of mine who happened to bring

Gerilyn to Chilangos one night about a year earlier. Because she said she wanted to learn how to bartend, I told Gerilyn the only

way to learn is to do it. At the time I really needed a bartender, so I hired her because I believed her desire would make it possible for her to learn fast. The night we met she drank too much and the next day she didn't remember our conversation. But Michelle kicked her that morning, and said, *Get up! You have to go to Leo's.*

What are you talking about? I'm not a bartender.

Michelle was pissed. She said, *You're not going to embarrass me in front of my friend Leo. You said you wanted a job and now you have to go.*

She called me to ask, *Do you really want me to come and work? I was only kidding about wanting a job.*

And I said, *But I wasn't.*

When she came to the restaurant I showed her everything behind the bar. I showed her the computer and said, *I'll see you later. If you have any questions, ask Tatiana or Diana. What was your name again?*

She said, *Gerilyn.*

Diana, Leo and Tatiana, with Olivia Wilson (daughter of Paul
and Denise Wilson) on St. Patrick's Day.

I said, *That sounds like the princess of Ireland. From now on you're Maria.*

When I went back that night, Gerilyn (aka Maria) apologized and said she couldn't work at Chilangos because half of the menu on the computer is in Spanish.

I said, *You can't leave. I need you. Think of it as an opportunity to learn Spanish.*

Every few days, for one reason or another, she would say, *Maybe I shouldn't work here.*

But I kept telling her she had to stay. I didn't know it at the time, but Maria needed me as much as I needed her. She told me why and gave me permission to share this story.

Her mother died when she was very young. She was raped by her neighbor and then her brother died a couple of years later. She was so depressed at one point and felt so worthless that she wanted to die, so she tried to kill herself by slashing her wrists, but she was discovered and taken to the hospital. From that point, her behavior was negative because she still felt worthless.

She told me one day about how I saved her life. Because she needed a sense of purpose and something to make her feel

Maria and Leo accepting the trophy for the Chili Contest, sponsored by the Highlands Business Partnership.

needed, working at Chilangos came at the perfect time and in a way, I was rescuing her from her past.

When I needed a manager for La Playa, I felt confident about hiring Maria. We had a stage built for live bands to play and people had a lot of fun there. Maria did an amazing job even with all of the nonsense that went on with the Freakstreak people. Maria had the right attitude and people skills to make it a success.

When summer was over, the Bruce Springsteen fan club from Barcelona was visiting like they did every so often. This time they were here because Bruce was touring and they would go to every concert in the tri-state area they could get tickets for. They came to Chilangos not only because they liked it, but because they knew it was one of Bruce's favorites. Jenny was excited when they offered us their two extra tickets to Met Life Stadium on September 19, 2012.

As we walked toward the field at the stadium, I noticed we were going right to the front of the stage. I said, *You guys should have told me we would be this close so I could bring a banner to say hello to El Jefe.*

243

So one of the girls with us went to the food court and got a piece of cardboard and a marker. Jenny asked, *What do you want me to write?*

I said, *How about "Chilangos in the house?"*

As I was looking up at the stage lined with instruments, I focused on Bruce, who was talking about life and death since Clarence Clemons had just died. He said that he believed that those who had passed, including Clarence and Danny Federici, the original keyboard player in the band, were in a better place. Then he suggested we should celebrate who was here and asked, *Who's in the house? The guitar man is in the house, the piano player is in the house....*

He went through the whole band introducing everyone that way. When he walked toward our side of the stage and saw us, he yelled, *Chilangos in the house!* After that, the band played, *Waitin' on a Sunny Day.*

After someone posted it on YouTube, my friends went crazy when they saw it because it was such wonderful advertising for Chilangos. The following month, the song *Waitin' on a Sunny Day* would have a deeper meaning for us, though we didn't know it at the time.

Jenny, Leo and members of the Bruce Springsteen Fan Club from Barcelona, at the concert.

Chilangos, post-Sandy, after renovations.

Chilangos After Sandy

In October, I had planned to go to Mexico to visit with Eric, my Mom and the rest of my family. My brother and his sons, Omar and Eduardo, run a small internet café they call Chilangos, downstairs off the garage. I also wanted to take my friend and co-writer, Yolanda, to show her where I grew up so she could see it for herself.

She wouldn't see the garbage dump I lived near since it had been cleaned up, but there was another one not too far away. I wanted her to experience Mexico for her own sake as well as for the sake of the book. But it wasn't the right time for her. Instead, I brought my niece Erika, who would appreciate seeing her family, especially Eric, her first cousin.

We had a nice trip, but when I called Jenny she told me about a storm that was headed our way. I hadn't heard anything about it because I wasn't watching the news. I wasn't too worried, but I was glad I would be back in time just in case anything happened.

Before I even got home Jenny had the windows boarded up. We weren't sure if it would be as bad as they were saying it would be, but just in case, we took the artwork off the walls at Chilangos, the Aztec calendar and the computers, and brought them home. We didn't have anywhere to evacuate to, but we thought we would be safe since our house sits on a hill about 30 feet above sea level.

My friend Ken Braswell and I were curious to see what was going on in town, so we drove around in my truck through the high winds and heavy rain. Trees had been blown down and there weren't too many other people out and about.

We were surprised to see a woman wearing a yellow raincoat walking around. We pulled up to talk to her. She was crying because she couldn't see through the wind and rain. She was lost and thanked us for rescuing her. We brought her to the shelter they had set up at Henry Hudson High School in town.

Soon we could see the water rising up not far from Chilangos and it wasn't long before about six feet of water filled up the street, tore up sidewalks and yards, and flooded houses, many that were already in bad shape. By the next morning, the town of Highlands looked war-torn as people emptied their houses full of wet things and piled them on the curbs.

The year before, we had Hurricane Irene, which wasn't nearly as bad, but bad enough that we shut down for a couple of days to deal with a little bit of damage. Sandy was another occasion to take the food meant for Chilangos and cook it elsewhere like I did during Irene, when I invited people to eat at my house. It would have been a crime to let all the food from the restaurant go to waste.

This time, since so many people were affected and really needed help, my plan was to set up in the Chilangos parking lot, cook in the trailer and feed anyone and everyone who came. I'd come a long way from my days of not having enough in Neza, but I still respected food as a precious thing that many people don't have. I told the Mayor of Highlands to tell everyone to come and eat. Instead, he told me to go to the shelter at the high school and use the kitchen there.

When I got there, there were two ladies who said they had been waiting for me. They were already making sandwiches, but I was invited to take over the kitchen. So I called everyone--- Jenny, Charly, Geovanny, Diana, Tatiana and Maria to come help me. We had shrimp, lobster, filet mignon and Mexican paella, and everyone was drooling. Danny Shields from the Windansea restaurant also sent food over when he heard I was cooking because they didn't want to waste it either. As it was ready, we put food on the pickup truck and went street by street in Highlands serving people whose houses had been destroyed.

We had enough donated food to cook for two weeks at the shelter. Even though Chilangos was also destroyed, there was nothing else we could do while we waited for insurance adjusters and FEMA officials to come take a look at our mess. Feeding people was our business, so instead of sitting around being upset, we did what we could out of the goodness of our hearts. It gave us a sense of purpose to use the ingredients that would have fed Chilangos' customers and transform the school into a four-star shelter.

I remembered seeing *Excalibur*, the 1981 movie about King Arthur, where a young man is chosen by the Gods to fight with a sword. Years later, when the war is over and he is the king sitting on his throne, something happens and he has to take the sword and fight again, which makes him feel alive. It seems that he needed that action to reawaken him by forcing him to use his talents. I'm not saying I was the king on a throne, but Hurricane Sandy came and punched me in the face and I had to fight to get my business back. I felt like that king because Sandy was the war that reawakened me.

Part of the consolation prize for Chilangos being shut down was the media recognition. The Today Show and Univision called and came to film the story. Other independent film-makers also wanted the scoop, not only about my business, but about the town in general. Every business had a decision to make in that moment that would affect the greater good of the entire town.

It made sense that the recurring question was, *Will Chilangos reopen?* We bring a lot of people into town who may not otherwise be there. Of course, before Sandy, there were several other restaurants doing well like Francesco's, The Inlet Café, Windansea, Bahr's, Moby's, The Taphouse, Grimaldi's, Bay Avenue Trattoria, The Clam Hut, Original Oyster, Off the Hook, The Lusty Lobster, The Chubby Pickle and the Bay Avenue Bakery & Café, and maybe one or two others I may have left out.

Together, we had all worked for years to build up the town and give people a reason to come and help it grow to the great shore town everyone wants it to be. I live in Highlands and love this town. That's why even though I wasn't sure how or when it would happen, there was no doubt in my mind that this would not be the end of Chilangos.

We cleaned up as much of the mess as we could before the insurance company would come to scope it out and made all the appropriate phone calls to FEMA and the bank. When there was nothing left to do, we realized we needed to decompress

251

from the situation. So we went to Florida for a family vacation. Getting away gave us a chance to gain some perspective and I remembered a very smart comment made by a Mexican man I admire. Carlos Slim, once the richest man in the world, said all crises are opportunities. It didn't take me more than a few hours to recognize Sandy as an opportunity because there were things we never would have had the chance to experience if Sandy hadn't clobbered us.

Danny Shields of Windansea escaped serious damage because the main dining area in his restaurant was situated higher than the water rose. Since they were able to re-open months before we were, he invited us to have Chilangos night there. He knew how many customers missed not only the food, but seeing their friends. It was a way to gather everyone and to help us make some money since we had been out of work and would be for a while longer. I knew people would come out to support us, but I had no idea how many. I was very pleasantly surprised by the line of people out the door. It was so crowded that even close friends, like Yolanda and her family, who couldn't wait for more than an hour to eat, didn't get in.

When it came time to rebuild, I was also pleasantly surprised by how many people responded to our offering of gift certificates that would become valid when we reopened. Then there were others who gave us loans like Daniel Morale, a customer who had become a friend. He walked in one day and said, *Oh my God, Leo, we have to get you back open. I was going to remodel my house with $50,000, but Chilangos is more important than my house. I'll give you the money.*

Mark Sharpe and my friend Pete Harris drove an hour to come help. Janny and Marco came and many other people helped us rebuild. Sherwin Williams in Middletown donated gallons of paint and even sent painters to help us. Friends also came to the door to ask what we needed and did whatever we asked them to do. It was truly a team effort of so many people who showed how much they care about us.

There were days when issues arose with either the bank or the insurance company. When I applied for an SBA loan to rebuild Chilangos several months had gone by before I found out the bank had misplaced the deed to the restaurant. They called to say if they didn't receive it that day I would have to reapply and wait another six months or longer. It was a crisis moment because I couldn't imagine another six months without Chilangos.

I didn't know what to do and got very agitated until I remembered just a week or two earlier, when I attended the meeting of the Latino Chamber of Commerce of Monmouth

County, where the New Jersey Lt. Governor, Kim Guadagno spoke to Sandy victims. To my amazement, she gave out her cell phone number for people to call in case they needed assistance. She said, *I work for you and you pay for this cell phone. You can call me any time and I will be there for you because that is my job.*

I didn't write the number down, but I knew if I called Luis Rodriguez, the Chamber president, he would give it to me. When I got it I immediately called Lt. Governor.

When she answered, I introduced myself as the owner of Chilangos and she said, *Oh, please tell me you're open.*

I said, *Not yet. I have a problem and I need your help.*

When she asked how she could help, I explained the story about needing the copy of the deed and she said, *OK and when do you need it?*

I said, *Today, 4 o'clock.*

She said, *I'll call you right back.*

Ten minutes later she called and said, *It's nice to have connections. I just talked to someone in Trenton and here's the number to call. She's going to pull your file that is all the way*

*at the bottom of the pile and email you the deed so you can
send it to the SBA in Texas. Is there anything else I can do for
you?*

I thought for two seconds. *Yes, there's one more thing. When I
have the re-opening of Chilangos, will you come and cut the
ribbon for me?*

She said, *Send me the invitation. I would love to be there.*

I was so happy I said, *Just imagine my life without you.*

She said, *You just made my day.*

I said, *No, you just made my life!*

A short time later, I was asked by a government official to
comment about my experience after Sandy. I told them about
Lt. Governor's response to my personal situation. They asked if
I would participate by telling my story in a TV commercial to
support Governor Christie's re-election. I agreed and a crew
came to Chilangos to film the commercial.

Eventually, I was invited to go with my family to the Governor's
Mansion for *Cinco de Mayo* and then later to Mexico City, to
the mansion where the United States Ambassador to Mexico
lived, with the Governor and other officials, and it made me
think about how far I had come. It took me three tries to get my

visa and now here I was eating finger food off silver platters in a beautiful mansion in my own country among many important people, including presidents and CEOs regarding commercial trading between Mexico City and New Jersey. People don't know, but there are 30,000 jobs that currently exist involving the trade industry between my current home state and my native home country.

My message to you right now is to build your future without forgetting where you are right now. It's a wonderful feeling to appreciate the journey you went on to get to where you decided you wanted to be.

Not in a very long time was there a better reason to celebrate than when we re-opened Chilangos in Highlands on June 6, 2013. As promised, Lt. Governor came to cut the ribbon, and we enjoyed music by our friend Tommy Grasso and ate at picnic benches set up in the Chilangos parking lot across the street. I had felt the same excitement as I did 11 years earlier when we first opened up. It was a catastrophe to have Chilangos destroyed and to have to put it back together, but it was an opportunity to rebuild it the way we really wanted it.

Now I am excited all over again because of the new décor and because so many people have expressed their enthusiasm and how bad they felt when we were shut down. It is rejuvenating for me personally and professionally, and reminds me what I set out to do when we first opened. That gives me so much power and energy. I use those moments during harder times. Right now, whatever people have to endure today, I wish for them to use it and trust that everything happens for a reason.

I have friends who come to Chilangos from Keansburg and have witnessed how a good business can bring people in and contribute to a town's viability. I got a call one day from the Mayor of Keansburg Tom Foley to tell me about all the business opportunities in his town that had also been devastated by Sandy.

He said, *I wanted to call you because we need you in our town. You have a good reputation, good food and you could be the spark we need here. Please come check it out.*

I wasn't negative, but I wasn't exactly positive either. But I said, *Yeah, I'll come see it.*

And he said, *No, really. You have to come.*

A few days later, I met Mayor Tom at Keansburg Borough Hall and he took me around in his pick-up truck. We drove down Ocean Avenue by a restaurant that I could tell was no longer in business. It was right across the street from the beach. When I asked Tom about it, he said, *It used to be a bar. It's a nice building and I'm pretty sure it's up for sale.*

There was no real estate sign on the property, but he said he would find out who owned it and connect us. I soon found out the price was right and started the process of making an offer. When the summer of La Playa in Highlands with Freakstreak had come to an end, I was sad and wondered how many tacos I'd have to sell to buy a beach and recreate the outdoor experience somewhere else. I didn't think I would ever have a restaurant across the street from the beach, but now I do.

When I asked Tom if I would be able to use the beach to have concerts, he said, *Anything you want, Leo. That's exactly why we want you.*

This was a lesson to always look for the opportunity in a crisis. Think about this. If you're upset or depressed about something, you shouldn't worry too much because you can count on one thing: It will change.

Another nearby garbage dump, officially called the *Bordo de Xochiaca* landfill, was one of the largest landfill sites in the Valley of Mexico and one of the dirtiest in the world. It began operating in the 1970s and contained about 12 million tons of trash. I wasn't still living there to see it happen (like I said, things change), but in the 2000s, it was finally closed and sealed. The 600 people who still lived there were relocated. The next thing they had to do was stabilize the ground and install a system to monitor and manage the gas produced by the rotting garbage. Then tubes were laid underground to collect the gases to produce fuel to generate electricity.

Carlos Slim and his billion-dollar company, Grupo Carso, started the project known as The Ciudad Jardín Bicentenario to make improvements for future generations. They built a shopping mall, campuses of the Universidad de La Salle, and a hospital. Apparently, the project has generated more than six thousand jobs. Talk about positive change!

I look back on my life so far, and I know things would have been different if my father had been there throughout my childhood, and I had gone to college. Maybe I would now have a small business in Mexico. Maybe I could have eventually had a bigger business in Mexico. But coming to the U.S. felt necessary to me for growth, for movement and change. It forced me to embrace a new culture, a different language and meet different people. I don't regret it.

The same proved to be true for my oldest son, Eric, who came to visit for the holidays in December 2013. There was so much to be grateful for and celebrate and I wanted him here as much as he wanted to be here. All five of us went to Florida for a break during the cold weather, but it followed us south and we froze in Florida. But it didn't matter. We enjoyed each other's company and he was happy. He would soon turn 17 and was starting to think about college. He had done very well in school in Mexico because he had already started taking classes that would prepare him for medical school to become a neurologist. But as he talked to people here about his goals and dreams, he was being told that he should consider going to college in the states. Because his mind was open, that quickly became his plan: To finish high school in Mexico and return to New Jersey for college. But with more conversations and more thought, we realized it would make more sense for him to finish high school in New Jersey before attempting to get into a college in the U.S.

With one more year left of high school, he applied to several undergraduate schools and was accepted to Monmouth University. I could not be more proud of him than I am.

I remember when he was younger and some of the talks we used to have. When he was 13, he asked me how you choose a mate. According to my experience, I said, *The first thing you do is understand that when you first meet someone, she's going to give you the best she has, even if she's not really that way all the time. You shouldn't focus on her as much as you should focus on her family and the kind of environment she grew up in. Was the mother a good mother, the father a good father? We tend to copy what our parents do, and if someone doesn't have good role models and you see problems within their family, then what can you expect from that person?*

Relationships are not easy. You're going to have differences. You're going to argue and fight. But it's normal. When you're in love you do stupid things. Once your heart gets involved with decisions, it can cause problems. I believe we are the most perfect thing that God has created. Our brains were created to think and determine and make decisions. Our hearts were created for something else other than that–feelings, but the minute your heart interferes with your brain's job, it can be disastrous. There are times when you shouldn't listen to your heart. It's important not to take things too seriously in life. It's just life.

There is so much I want to share with my children, which is one very important reason I've been working on this book. It's about communication. Sure, I talk to them, but reading about someone's life and perspective is different. Communication is so important. The one thing I can say about me–I am the best at understanding people. I can say it. I could scream it. I am hoping all my children have the same gift.

I listened and remembered when my third-grade teacher said I had the ability to listen and observe. I don't remember why she said it, but I remember her saying it. It was true. I know how to listen to people. When I listen to you, I listen with my eyes, my mind, my ears and a lot of times, my heart is focusing on you. Sometimes people hear you talking, but they aren't listening. When somebody is trying to communicate, I lean in because I want to understand. You can learn a lot by listening.

I'm always talking to my kids and asking them questions to make them think. One day, I asked them if they had the opportunity to thank God for something right now, what would it be.

It took Gabriela two seconds to say, *My beautiful family.*

Emiliano said, *My food and my life.*

It's important to be aware of the gifts you have. Recognizing the good in your life will help you not to focus on whatever isn't perfect. Every day think about what you're grateful for and it will make you happier, if even for a moment. You may not have a lot of money, but I've realized that money isn't the most important thing in life.

Money has never been an issue even when we didn't have any. As a dishwasher I made $300 a week working seven days a week. My rent was only $200 a month. I didn't have a car; I had a bicycle. I didn't smoke. I didn't spend money at the mall and I would eat at work. Therefore, I was able to save money.

In Mexico, I didn't get a paycheck. I was working for the family cause, but when I needed something I would take money from the cash register at the end of the night when we were counting it. Since my Mom knew the money would be spent on something important, like shoes or clothing, she didn't ask questions.

Money is not really that important to me. I like when I have it, but it's not everything. You don't have to have money to be rich. My Mom's family, who were the poorest ones of all, are now the most successful. My brother Eduardo works construction and just opened up his own restaurant in Long Branch with his wife, Lorena. My other brother Alejandro in Mexico has kids who go to the university. My sister Noemi is married to a principal of a school in Mexico City. They don't have a lot of money, but they are comfortable. We are all comfortable. Other people I know who have been given everything rather than having to work for it are a mess. I happen to know a lot of poor people who have nothing but money. Whatever you do, don't think about money. If you want to know what to do to make money, think of what you like doing. Think about what gives you joy. I love to talk. I love to have friends. I love tequila. I love food. And guess what? For all of that, I get paid. I don't think about money. I think about what I'm going to do and how I'm going to enjoy it.

Yet, I am still proud that the richest man in the world is Mexican. Even though Carlos Slim is worth about $72 billion, he lives in Mexico in the same house he bought about 30 years ago. He made his money by taking over companies that were in trouble, like Sears and CompUSA, and turning them around. I like him because he believes that your intelligence is not always a product of your education. It's about knowing what you should do and when you should do it. We have that in common. I am certainly not worth billions, but I feel like I am, which is more important than anything else. You're only as lucky as you think you are.

Fun family portrait taken at Six Flags of (top, far
left) Ulises and Diana Fragoso, Gabriela, Eric, Jenny, Emiliano,
and Leo.

Leo (far left), cousin Yolanda, niece Lisette, sister-in-law
Victoria, brother Alejandro and nephew Omar. Leo's nephew
Eduardo wasn't with us that day.

My friend, Julio Moreno, who was a production assistant and also had a small part in the movie, "Maria Full of Grace" (2004) learned how fortunate he is the hard way. He used to be a TV reporter in Colombia and well-known in the Latino world. A few years back, he had a video recording device, which he took apart late at night, trying to fix it. When he got up in the morning, one of the screws from the machine was on the floor, and he stepped on it and it went into his foot. It hurt and the doctor gave him medicine for the condition it created called cellulitis.

A few days later, his foot turned black. The doctor said they would have to amputate. He spent 11 months in the hospital and lost his leg up to his knee. Before they amputated, Julio asked the doctor if he could first go home. He didn't say anything, but he was planning to kill himself. Then he met an up-and-coming basketball player who had gotten electrocuted and lost both arms and both legs. Suddenly, he felt grateful that he only lost part of one leg.

The best we can do, like Eleanor Roosevelt said, is push past our fears and do the things we think we can't do. I used to go to the World Trade Center in an attempt to fight my fear of heights. I couldn't get too close to the window, but I tried so many times, thinking that one day I would conquer it. Because the towers were knocked down, I wasn't able to finish the job. The point is that I tried and kept trying. That is what I do. I'm afraid of so many things, but fighting them is the only way to grow and be successful.

So many things have happened and continue to happen that I would like to document. One day I was thinking about how to pull it all together and it hit me. We could do a docu-reality show following the progress of everything we do including the restaurants, JannyMarco's musical endeavors, the book and maybe even a movie. I'd also like to document taking groups of people around the world, especially to Mexico, to see what it's really like.

We would also take mission trips to different countries where people need help, and make that part of the show. One of the first places I'd like to go is Colombia to help children who are indirect victims of AIDS. We would bring them toys, cook for them and chip in for Father Bernard of Bogota, who builds houses.

I'd also like to provide people in other poverty-stricken parts of the world with the resources to start small businesses so they may become self-sustaining. It would be a great way for people to see different countries and give back at the same time. From that perspective, we want to help the ones who want to help the ones who need help.

Not too long ago, Yolanda and I met with Janice Selinger, a 13-time Emmy Award-winning documentary producer, and Esther Novak, the founder and CEO of VanguardComm, a multi-cultural marketing firm, to talk about how to get our docu-realty show made. They also brought with them Diego Maya from Colombia, someone else who is pursuing his dream of producing a TV show called *Latino Spirit* to document Latinos who are making a difference. We became instant friends because he is proof that if you think positive thoughts, you bring positive things into your life.

One day when we were at Chilangos, Geovanny came from the kitchen to tell me we were out of green tomatillos. I said I would run to the Long Branch grocery store to buy some and took Diego along so we could continue talking about the pilot for the reality show I want to do revolving around the life and times of a Chilango. I am fortunate to have people like Diego, who have the same kind of motivation and dedication to his work in TV and film, show up unexpectedly in my life.

When we got to the store there was a young Mexican lady standing outside with a small cooler and a piece of cardboard that said, "Tamales." I asked Diego if he was hungry. He shrugged, but I wanted to buy some tamales not only to try them out, but because I wanted to support her. I asked how much. She said four for $7. She had chicken in green tomatillo sauce or pork in *mole* (mo-leh) sauce. I asked for two each and handed her $10.

When we got back to the kitchen at Chilangos, I took one green and one mole tamal and unwrapped the corn husk and gave Diego a fork. He tried them and he made a happy face because he thought they were really good. I knew they were good, but I also knew they could be better.

With tongs I piled some shredded chicken breast that I used for my burritos and placed it on top, followed by a ladle of green tomatillo sauce, cilantro and sour cream. Diego loved it.

I did the same thing with the pork and mole sauce. I placed pork on top, mole sauce and garnished with sour cream and cilantro and totally changed the look of the tamales. I had Diego try them again and he went bananas. He said, *You not only changed the way they look, but the flavor is amazing.*

Tamales are not on the regular menu at Chilangos because I don't like to reheat them. When they get dried out they're not as good.

I said, *I think I just invented something: Naked Tamales.*

Diego said, *That name sounds so commercial.*

We looked it up immediately to find out if it was already trademarked and it was not. So guess who trademarked it? I decided I could even have different toppings like shrimp, lobster, short ribs, ground beef and raisins, barbecued pulled pork and coconut coleslaw, crab meat and tilapia *a la* Veracruzana, among other things.

I have already gotten got in touch with the EDA and UCEDC to talk about funding and the creation of a franchise. If you live in New Jersey, you can look for a Naked Tamales truck, try them and see what you think.

I have a secret, but I didn't know it until people started asking me, Leo, why are you always happy? What's your secret? I will tell you. It's not really a secret. We all think differently about success. I've learned so many things about how to live in an almost constant state of motivation and inspiration. I will share them with you. It has to do with attitude. Something that drives me crazy is when a new idea is presented and the reasons it can't work are the first suggestions.

The Naked Tamales food truck. Special thanks to our friend
Ed Gabel for the beautiful logo.

I never know what I'm going to dream up next, but whatever it is, I'm open to it. If it doesn't work that's probably because something better is going to happen instead. But I like to find these things out myself. I don't want to be told what it's like to have an experience. I want to experience it, even the bad times that aren't fun when they're happening. If it wasn't for all the things I've been through, I wouldn't be here telling my story, nor would I have a story to share. But I have learned time and time again that keeping an open mind never fails to create some action that is positive at least part of the time.

I have always wanted to break a Guinness World Record by making the largest enchilada in the world, but that hasn't happened yet and it's not an easy thing to do. It occurred to me that each time we open a Naked Tamales in some form---mobile food truck, a store or even a kiosk---we could make a large tamal to celebrate the grand opening, starting with a 10-foot long tamal and growing it by one foot every time we open a new store.

When Naked Tamales becomes a franchise, it will be fun and meaningful for me to give people an opportunity to enter the entrepreneurial world---a world of headaches, stress, excitement, satisfaction and victory, if you know how to get there.

I think it's going to be very successful for anyone who is willing to work. Isn't that the most important thing in life? I'm talking about the willingness to relate to and help people, to work hard and also to have fun. That is what my mother taught me. She is 74 years old and when she plays with my kids, she becomes a kid. She is the most beautiful thing in my life. If it wasn't for my Mom I wouldn't be who I am. If the way I feel is because of the "microchip" of optimism (in spite of poverty) my mother planted inside me, it worked for me and I feel gifted. If it wasn't for where I come from, I may not be as happy as I am right now. My Mom's life has been about helping people grow and reach their goals, and she passed that on to me.

Abigail, also known as Abuelita, taken by Nancy Kravis.

Yolanda's view of Las Pyramedes de Teotihuacán, the ancient Pyramids built by the Mayans.

Chilangos Tours

Here's one more piece of advice from a Chilango. Don't die without seeing Mexico. And I'm not talking about watching YouTube videos. You have to see the real thing to fully appreciate it.

About half a million Americans have discovered Mexico to be an incredibly magical country to live in or visit. My beloved Mexico City, which was built on a reservoir and has been sinking very slowly ever since, is now considered to be one of the hottest travel destinations in the world. When we first started working on the book, I was frustrated because so many people let their assumptions and fear about Mexico City keep them in the dark. It bothered me because I was taught to face my fears.

There is crime, but not enough to stop the millions of tourists who visit. Think of New York City, a busy, relatively dangerous place because of the traffic and dense population. Yet it is alive every single day with people who don't let either reported or unreported crime prevent them from seeing a Broadway show or bike-riding in Central Park. There is common sense and there is fear. Not going to New York because of the possibility of terrorist attacks, or Mexico because of the cartels, is an example of letting fear limit your experience.

Poverty and drug- and cartel-related crimes are the biggest problems there, but the poor people of Mexico City are more focused on their survival than causing trouble for other people, especially tourists. The government doesn't tolerate crimes against tourists because they rely so heavily on tourism for the overall survival of the country. They can't afford for you not to go back, or for you to go home and tell your friends what a dangerous place Mexico City is and why they shouldn't go there.

Drugs and cartel-related crime hasn't always been an issue. There was always a degree of corruption, which exists just about everywhere, but it was about 16 years ago that Mexico City—which happens to be the oldest city in North America--- was considered one of the most violent cities in the world. More specifically, Juarez was called one of the most dangerous places on earth. Before drugs became such a problem, criminals were very busy robbing banks. More recently, it's all about drugs, which accounts for $40 billion a year and 40 percent of the corruption of Mexico. Mexicans who resent these sad facts believe American drug use directly feeds the monster and often express that by saying, "The closer we are to the United States, the farther we are from God."

Regardless of that, I am equally proud to be Mexican as I am to be American, which wasn't an easy thing to accomplish. I may not have been able to honestly say I'm proud to be from either country if I had not experienced both to this extent. Everything is relative and now I have perspective and appreciation for both. I realize how fortunate that is and how many people never leave their home states, never mind the country, again, because of fear. There is plenty of ignorance, but I believe it's better to live with an open mind and accept how much you don't know, and do whatever you can to change that.

There are so many interesting things people don't know about the United Mexican States (its official name). But first I have to tell you, if you didn't already know, the first language spoken in the U.S. was not English. It was *español*!

The first Europeans to settle in North America spoke Spanish. According to the 2007 American Community Survey conducted by the United States Census Bureau, Spanish is the first language of more than 34 million people. More than 45 million Latin people live in the U.S. This is not to say we are taking over, but we are most definitely a prominent force in this country. Equally important to consider is the fact that about one million Americans live in Mexico, a popular place to retire, especially for Canadians as well as Americans.

Travelers are attracted to Mexico because the landscape is not just beaches or city streets; it's so diverse. There are culturally rich college towns and town squares where music plays in the streets (not just mariachis), and artists display their work. Monarch butterflies take their annual flight from the U.S. and Canada to land in Mexico, where there are long stretches of highway that separate the city from farmland, and small farming towns, mountains, pyramids, natural springs and volcanoes. Mexico is a great choice for you if you want to live comfortably for less money in a warm climate.

Now more than ever, I enjoy visiting Mexico City and the surrounding areas, especially when I have the chance to bring friends with me. I love to show off the beauty of the landscape, the people and the culture and mostly to show them how different it is from what they expected it to be. The islands of Mexico that people tend to visit—Cancun, Acapulco and Cabo San Lucas---are very beautiful places to vacation, but the real Mexico cannot be discovered at a resort. The folklore, a combination of food, the music, the way people live simply but passionately represent a festive culture unlike any other.

Mariachi is one of the gifts of Mexican culture with an interesting history. The word mariachi means party day or *dia de fiesta* in Otomi, the language of the Jalisco region of Mexico where tequila originated. The word was coined when the French settled in Mexico, where the natives worked for the French on their farms. The Mexicans were curious about the French people's parties and the reasons behind them. They were mainly weddings. The French word for wedding is *marriage*. Because of the language barrier, the Mexicans took the word *marriage* and turned it into mariachi, and created the style of music and dress and adapted them to their own celebrations. Mariachi is known all over the world, yet Mexico is also famous for introducing other things to the rest of the world like chocolate, tacos, enchiladas, burritos and tamales. Tequila is the national drink, but hot chocolate was the sacred drink of the Aztecs.

The food at Chilangos is very important to me, but equally important is our tequila bar. Chilangos has been recognized by the *New York Times* as having the largest tequila selection on the east coast because we offer more than 275 different brands.

One of the places I'd like to take someone who appreciates tequila is the agave fields and to visit a distillery, like my friends who make the brand Alma De Agave tequila in Jalisco. Drinking tequila is beautiful, but it's even better to understand how it is made, how it became such a huge part of our culture and why it became the number one alcohol in the world. Wouldn't you like to see for yourself what it takes to create a good brand of tequila?

One day, I will create Chilangos tequila with Mr. Jalapeno Pepper as the bottle, which will be *blanco* and jalapeno-infused. It reminds me of when my wife was pregnant and I had to wait for the baby to be born so I could hold him or her in my arms. I'm still waiting to hold that precious bottle of Chilangos tequila.

If you don't already appreciate tequila, maybe it's because you had a bad experience that led you to believe that tequila is bad for you. It might help you to know that any tequila that is impure---meaning it isn't 100-percent agave---is bad for you because it has unnecessary chemicals and sugars that take the place of the agave. It's no different from getting sick because you've mixed alcohols. Under Mexican law, tequila must be made from the Blue Weber agave plant grown only in the state of Jalisco. If you drink high quality tequila in moderation and plenty of water to stay hydrated, you should not get a hangover or feel sick in any way. That is the good news.

The bad news is, as my friend Nene Gonzalez, president of Alma De Agave Tequila, says, you can't believe every label that claims to be 100-percent agave because the Mexican government allows eight percent to be used for artificial coloring, flavoring and infusions. According to Nene, Alma is "old school" and "beyond organic" because their product is so pure.

Unless you want a headache, don't buy tequilas containing chemicals or additives like coloring, or mezcal with the worm in it. As long as you follow those general rules, tequila can actually be good for you. It's the only alcohol that is considered a stimulant rather than a depressant. They say a shot before you eat can stimulate your appetite. If you drink it after you eat, it helps digestion. Some people believe it can even lower your cholesterol and it can certainly help you relax. But you can't go crazy with it. Treat it well and it will treat you well.

I've been asked over and over again to name the best tequila. The answer is this: The best tequila is the one you like best. There is no such thing as the best tequila. Someone could call a particular brand "the best," but if you don't like it, you won't call it the best no matter what anyone else says. Doesn't that make sense?

There are so many different brands to choose from--categorized by age, flavor and price. Tequila that has not been aged is called

Blanco (also called silver) and is colorless. If it has been aged in oak barrels between two months and one year, it is called *Reposado* and is usually a light gold color or sometimes light pink. *Añejo* (meaning vintage) is aged in oak barrels between one and three years.

I've been known to use tequila in recipes, which isn't unusual, unless you use it in desserts. In 2011, town officials asked me to represent Highlands at the Six Flags Grape Adventure (Battle of the Chefs) at Six Flags Great Adventure in Jackson Township. To enter we had to go there and feed 50 guests and three judges. It pushed me out of my comfort zone because I wasn't used to having to talk about my food while serving. Part of the process was for the judges to interview each chef about their style and presentation.

It made me happy when one of the judges said our food was unbelievably delicious and fresh. It made me ecstatic when I was told how charismatic I was. It also made me laugh because I knew that I was being funny because I was so nervous. If I was calm, I might not have been as entertaining as I served barbecued pulled pork and coconut coleslaw tamales (future Naked Tamales) as the appetizer, *Poblano* peppers stuffed with chicken, almonds, raisins, plantains and pineapple as the entrée and *tres leches* (three milks) cake for dessert. It wasn't your ordinary *tres leches* cake though because I had a brainstorm one day while Jenny and I were at Chilangos making the cake.

When it was finished baking I wanted to see what it would taste like with a splash of Alma de Agave Reposado tequila on top. When I tried it I said, *Oh my God. This is it!*

The following week I put it on my specials menu and it sold very well. By the end of the night that weekend, a few of my friends came in and asked about "the tequila cake."

They said, *Give us one with tequila and one without so we can taste the difference.*

They loved both, but they thought it was *muy especial* with the tequila.

I said, *This is nothing. Wait until you see what I'm working on next.* Joking, on the spot, I said, *I'm creating a tres leches margarita.*

They were drooling. I almost said I was only kidding, but instead, I went to the kitchen and took two scoops of vanilla ice cream, a slice of cake and went back to the bar. I took the blender and I said, *You are about to witness my latest invention.*

285

I put the cake inside the blender with the ice cream and counted to six as I poured the tequila. Then I counted to three while I poured Triple Sec. I blended it and poured it into shot glasses. Once we all did a shot, everyone was screaming because they loved it. And cake shots were born! Now I serve them when good friends come in.

As we waited for the results of the Battle of the Chefs, I had a good feeling. I knew everyone loved me as a person, but I saw so many beautiful dishes and fancy presentations with things like flowers, so I wasn't sure what to expect. I didn't really care whether or not I won. Just being there and making new friends and making people happy made me feel like a winner.

A few minutes later, the judges came out and announced the first place winner was Chilangos Restaurant, Leo Cervantes. Then Bugs Bunny and Tweetie Bird came over to congratulate us. We got a certificate, a full year of advertising on the Great Adventure website and 30 tickets to Six Flags. That moment of victory tasted as good as a shot of top-shelf tequila.

That was some tangent I got lost on, but that's how tequila works sometimes. My original point was the many reasons to visit Mexico. For people who have never been there and don't know, Mexico isn't a dusty little place, but rather a beautiful, diverse country with something for everyone. For decades it's had the reputation as a place to avoid because of the high crime rate, other than for the resorts. But what they don't tell you is tourists are safer in Mexico than natives. Like I said before, the reason is because the Mexican government wants to improve their reputation and protect it by cracking down on crimes that target non-Mexicans.

Like traveling anyplace you've never been, it's best to have a tour guide to get the full spectrum of what the country has to offer. I am a great tour guide because I know it so well. For me, it's like being on vacation and so much more because I'm still so connected to the culture, the traditions and the people. I know where to go and where not to go. Some of the most enjoyable sites in Mexico are things you can't find anywhere else. I am going to name some, but this is certainly not a complete list. These are the things that stand out in my opinion as reasons to take an Interjet flight and see what I'm talking about.

1. The Basilica of Our Lady of Guadalupe is a religious site in Mexico City where every year people from all over the world show up to be part of the celebration of the Virgin of Guadalupe, who is said to have appeared December 12, 1531. That was almost 500 years ago, yet seven million people still go to the site that day expecting, or at least hoping the same vision appears to them as she was said to have appeared to St. Juan

Diego Cuauhtlatoatzin, an Aztec convert to Roman Catholicism. In 2002, the Pope made Juan Diego the first Mexican saint. You see the original apron with the image of the Virgin hanging at the Basilica. The Catholic faith has amazing strength in Mexico.

My family has never been religious. We believe in God, but not the God that you see in the pictures because that was before cameras were invented. God exists, but I see it in different things. God is the air we breathe, in the sun, the moon, the stars, etc. I feel that God is energy. I believe people see and hear what they need to see and hear. Seventy-five percent of my brain believes that the Virgin of Guadalupe was a creation of the Spaniards when they came to conquer Mexico to make the natives fearful and therefore surrender. The other 25 percent of my brain wants to see and hear what everybody else believes in, and be captivated by a spiritual moment in time.

2. The *Museo Nacional de Antropología* (National Anthropological Museum) in Mexico City contains one of the best collections of historical artifacts in its 23 exhibition halls. The museum is located in Chapultepec Park, one of the largest city parks in the world, where there is so much to do and see. I remember hearing the names of places when I was little–like Teotichuacan, Chapultapec, Chichenitza and Xochimilco, and

because I didn't know what they were I thought they sounded funny. As I grew up and learned the meanings of the names and places, I realized we're Mexicans, but we're also Spanish from Spain. I identify more with the Aztec Mexican than Spaniard because of their overall beliefs about how the gods, humans and nature are interconnected.

When you begin to understand who you are and where you come from, going to a place like the Museum of Anthropology provides proof of your culture and history right in front of you.

The most famous of the museum's exhibits is the Stone of Axayacatl, the real Aztec calendar made of stone. If you come to Chilangos, you'll see a replica hanging on the wall. I also have one in my house. It depicts the sun god Tonatiuh, the symbol of the Fifth World, according to Aztec mythology. I guess you could say it's my crucifix. For one thing it's beautiful décor, but more importantly, it's a symbol of Mexican culture I want my children to recognize and feel connected to.

3. You must see *Las Pyramedes de Teotihuacán* (teh-oh-tee-wa-KHAN), if you appreciate ruins, about 30 miles northeast of Mexico City.

I have been there to climb the Pyramid of the Sun (the third largest pyramid in the world) and the Pyramid of the Moon about 10 times in my life. When I've been at the top I definitely felt something, a sense of relief. It could be because of the altitude. Whatever it is depends what you believe in.

Teotihuacán means "place where gods were born," reflecting what the Aztecs believed---that the gods created the universe here around 300 AD, with these monuments constructed on geometric and symbolic principles.

4. The Mayans' *Cenote Sagrado*, which means "sacred well" in Spanish, can be found at the pre-Columbian Mayan archaeological site of Chichenitza, in the northern Yucatán Peninsula. People and things like gold, jade and pottery were sacrificed into the sacred well (*cenote*) as a way of worshipping Chaac, the Mayan rain god. It's a center of pure energy provided directly by our own Mother Nature.

5. Guadalajara is Mexico's second largest city, where two things I love---mariachi music and tequila---come from. It's also known for its industry and business, and is sometimes called Mexico's Silicon Valley. In the 1950s, new buildings and shopping centers were built, but there are still many old beautiful buildings left to see. If you like shopping, you should definitely visit *el Mercado Libertad* as well as Tlaquepaque and Tonala.

6. Latin America has always been famous for carnivals. But one of the largest is El Carabal Carnival in Mazatlan, which happens five days before Ash Wednesday in March. There's also the Malicon Motorcycle Week in Mazetlan, which is one of the largest gathering places of motorcycles anywhere. Imagine yourself in a place where just about everyone there is seeking the freedom of motorcycle riding. I've never been to the carnival, but it is definitely on my list.

7. Another experience similar to the carnival, where you can enjoy the arts is the annual *Festival Cervantino* in Guanajuato City, where my parents were born and raised. You could say it's the most important festival representing the arts and culture of Mexico held in October. It originated in the mid-20th century when Miguel de Cervantes, who wrote *Don Quixote*, had some of his short plays performed in the city's plazas. I am proud to have the same name as the man who wrote the first novel.

8. There's a majestic archaeological park in Riviera Maya in Cancun called *Xcaret*, where there's a show to see with hundreds of actors on stage taking you on a musical journey through the history of Mexico. There you can also see the coral reef aquarium, a pre-Hispanic ball game recreated, ruins, a butterfly pavilion, beaches and natural pools where you can swim with dolphins. This is another magical Mexican place

where Mother Nature has created something for us to enjoy and admire.

9. If you visit Mexico during *Cinco de Mayo*, it's most fitting to go to Puebla City, since it's actually a celebration of the Battle of Puebla, not Mexico's Independence Day, which happens to be September 16. Cinco de Mayo celebrates Mexico's fight against Napoleon and the French invasion of Mexico. May 5, 1862 marks the victorious Battle of Puebla.

10. There are a lot of amazing things in Mexico City, such as *Torre Mayor*, the strongest building in Latin America, recognized in the Guinness Book of World Records. Located at *Paseo de la Reforma*, the former location of the *Cine Chapultepec*, Canadian-owned Reichmann International Construction began building it in 1999, reaching completion in late 2003. At 738 feet tall and 57 stories, it was designed to stand up against the kind of earthquakes Mexico City is prone to, such as the one in 1985 when I was 16. It registered 8.1 on the Richter scale, which would have been OK for *Torre Mayor* because it can support a quake registering 9.0. You definitely want to be inside a building with that kind of strength during an earthquake.

By then, we had upgraded the cardboard roof of our house to concrete, which is what most houses were made of at the time. I was sleeping when my oldest sister Noemi walked into the room and shook me awake. She said, *Don't be afraid.*

Of what? I asked.

Then I heard the house cracking in every corner. She said, *Esta temblando!*

I got up and walked out of the house onto the street. By then, there were also new sidewalks. I watched as they popped up from the ground like they would in a movie. The electric poles were swaying back and forth like they were made of rubber. The sky turned dark purple and blue. One thing I will never forget were the dogs howling and barking. It was very scary. I watched people on their knees praying in the streets. They were disoriented. The ground seemed to be rocking. There was nowhere to go and hide and nothing to do, other than to wait and see what was going to happen. We found out that Mexico City was devastated and more than 10,000 people died within minutes.

In spite of the difficulties we dealt with, we have also had so much good fortune. I am grateful every day for the people I work with and others who surround me. We are all lucky to have such a colorful culture with a popular cooking and eating style that's both fun and festive, and sought after by so many people. Otherwise, I might not have such success with my Mexican restaurants---Chilangos and *La Playa*---full of fun-loving clientele who have become my friends over the years, as well as my catering business and mobile kitchen.

The Chilangos food truck.

Customers are attracted by the spices in the food, the peppers, the sauces, tequila, celebrations like *Cinco de Mayo* and the music. My job, as I see it, is to bring Mexico to the United States by combining the best of all of these things with my own inventions.

Now I must ask you an important question. Are you interested in visiting Mexico? Maybe you have never been, but have formed opinions about it. Or maybe you have never considered it a travel destination because you have heard it's dangerous.

Have you already gone, but weren't that impressed? Keep in mind how easy it is to visit one small corner of a country for a week and think you can classify it based on that isolated place, time and experience. Before coming to any conclusions, I encourage you to go with me to see the real Mexico and embrace the culture that excites me and inspires me every step of the way. Life is short. I believe in turning dreams into reality.

Whether it's running a restaurant or a night club, rebuilding a restaurant after a hurricane, becoming part of the music world as a manager, filming a reality TV show, trying to figure out how to make the largest enchilada in the world, building a franchise, organizing a tour group or writing a book, or whatever else you may be inspired to do, I encourage you to do it. Start right now!

I'm serious about taking you to Mexico. If you want to go, just ask me and we'll make it happen.

Viva Mexico! And God Bless America.

Made in the USA
Middletown, DE
26 May 2016